THE ETHICAL SLUT

THE ETHICAL SLUT

A GUIDE TO INFINITE
SEXUAL POSSIBILITIES

DOSSIE EASTON &
CATHERINE A. LISZT

greenery press

Cover illustration by Kai Harper.

Cover design by DesignTribe, San Francisco.

Published in the United States by Greenery Press, 3739 Balboa Ave. #195, San Francisco, CA 94121.

E-mail: verdant@crl.com

http://www.bigrock.com/~greenery

ISBN 0-890159-01-8

Table of Contents

ACKNOWLEDGMENTS

Many, many thanks for the information and encouragement we received from:

Cecelia & Corwin	Sunny Knight
Betty Dodson	Adric Petrucelli
Jaymes Easton	Carol Queen
Francesca Guido	Maggi Rubenstein
Lizzard Henry	Ruth & Edward
Sybil Holiday	Doug Stinson
Ron Hoffman	Susan S.
Richard Karpinsky	Snow White
Laurie & Chris	Tom & Katy
Deirdre McGrath	Joi Wolfwomyn

From Dossie

to Jim Garver, who made the space for me to learn

and

Kai Harper, my beloved and outrageous partner in love and in life

From Catherine

to Barbara, with love and gratitude

and

to Jay, my hun – finally and always

PART I – WITHIN OURSELVES

CHAPTER 1. WHO IS AN ETHICAL SLUT?

Many people dream of living an open sexual life — of having all the sex and love and friendship they want. Most never try, believing that such a life is impossible. Of those who try, many give up, finding the challenges insurmountable — or at least too hard for them. A few persist, and discover that being openly sexual and intimate with many people is not only possible, but can be more rewarding than they ever imagined.

People have been succeeding at free love for many decades — often quietly, without much fanfare. In this book, we will share the techniques, the skills, the ideals that have made it work for them.

So who is an ethical slut? We are. Many, many others are. Maybe you are too. If you dream of freedom, if you dream of sex, if you dream of an abundance of friends and flirtation and consensual conquest, of following your desires and seeing where they take you, you've already taken the first step.

Why We Chose This Title

From the moment you saw or heard about this book, you probably guessed that some of the terms here may not have the same meanings you're accustomed to.

What kind of person would revel in calling himself a slut? And why would he insist on being recognized for his ethics?

In most of the world, "slut" is a highly offensive term, used to describe a woman whose sexuality is voracious, indiscriminate and shameful. It's interesting to note that the analogous word "stud," used to describe a highly sexual man, is often a term of approval and envy. If you ask about a man's morals, you will probably hear about his honesty, loyalty, integrity and high principles. When you ask about a woman's morals, you are more likely to hear about who she fucks and under what conditions. We have a problem with this.

So we are proud to reclaim the word "slut" as a term of approval, even endearment. To us, a slut is a person of any gender who has the courage to lead life according to the radical proposition that *sex is nice and pleasure is good for you.* A slut may choose to have sex with herself only, or with the Fifth Fleet. He may be heterosexual, homosexual or bisexual, a radical activist or a peaceful suburbanite.

As proud sluts, we believe that sex and sexual love are fundamental forces for good — activities with the potential to strengthen intimate bonds, enhance lives, create spiritual awareness, even change the world. And, furthermore, we believe that all consensual sexual choices have these potentials — that any sexual pathway, consciously chosen and mindfully followed, can be a positive, creative force in the lives of individuals and their communities.

A slut shares his sexuality the way a philanthropist shares her money — because they have a lot of it to share, because it makes them happy to share it, because sharing makes the world a better place. Sluts often find that the more sex and love they give away, the more they have — a loaves-and-fishes miracle in which greed and generosity go hand-in-hand to provide more for everybody. Imagine living in sexual abundance!

SEXUAL ADVENTUROUSNESS

The world generally views sluts as debased, degraded, promiscuous, indiscriminate, jaded, immoral adventurers, destructive, out of control and driven by some form of psychopathology that prevents them from entering into a healthy monogamous relationship. Oh, yes, and definitely not ethical.

We see ourselves as people who are committed to finding a place of sanity with sex, and to freeing ourselves to enjoy our sexuality and to share it in as many ways as may fit for each of us. We may not always know what fits without trying it on, so we tend to be curious and adventurous. When we see someone who intrigues us, we like to be free to respond, and in exploring our own response, discover whatever is special about that person we are turned on to. We like relating to people, and tend to be gregarious, enjoying the company of different sorts of folk, and reveling in how our differences expand our horizons and offer us new ways to be ourselves.

Sluts tend to want a lot of things: different forms of sexual expression, different people, perhaps men and women both. We are curious: what would it be like to combine the energies of four or five people in one incandescent sexual encounter? What would it be like to share physical intimacy with that person who has been my best friend for ten years? What would it be like with this other person who is so very different from me? Some of us express more than one identity in intimate encounters with diverse people. Some of us love flirtation for its own sake, as an art form, and others make an art form out of sex. All of us love adventure.

When Dossie was a young adult, and not yet aware of herself as a slut, she found herself fascinated by people from all the different cultures she could find in urban America, and used to describe her sexual curiosity as her own idiosyncratic form of cross-cultural anthropology.

> *I delighted in finding people who were new and different: I learned an enormous amount from people who grew up in cultures that were more emotionally and sexually expressive than mine was, or who could see beauty in places I had never looked before. I'd grown up in a small monocultural town in New England, very rigid, lily white, WASPish. In the exploration of otherness I found answers to many of the dilemmas of my programming, or my culture-bound thinking: new ways I could be that worked better for me.*

Dossie certainly took a lot of risks in her reckless exploration of all the different sexualities she could find in New York City. For her, it was worth it. For some of us, sluttishness is a basic part of our identity, how we know ourselves.

One of the most valuable things we can learn from open sexual lifestyles is that our programming is changeable. Starting by questioning all the ways we have been told our sexuality ought to be, we can begin to edit and rewrite our old tapes. So by breaking the rules, we both free and empower ourselves.

Catherine remembers learning that there was such a thing as a gay man:

> *I must have been eight or nine, but even then, I understood the subtext of what I was hearing — that these men didn't belong in my comfortable suburban environment, that they had sex with each other in spite of the fact that many people thought it was wrong for*

them to do so, that they didn't necessarily get married and only have sex with one person, that they had their own communities where they hung out together and took care of each other because regular people didn't want them around. And I immediately got this strong sense of 'Oh, people like me.' Two decades went by before I came out as a slut, and another decade before I came out as bisexual, but there was something about the whole idea that I simply understood and responded to deep in my gut.

A SLUT'S EYE VIEW

What does this all look like from the slut's point of view? We see ourselves first and foremost as individuals, with virtues and faults and diverse differences. We are people who like sex, and who like many diverse kinds of people. We are not necessarily sexual athletes — although we do tend to train more than most. But good sex is not contingent on setting world records. We value sex for the pleasure it brings us, and the good times we get to share with however many wonderful people.

We love adventure. Once again, in some contexts the word adventurer is pejorative, suggesting that the adventurous person is immature or ungenuine, not really willing to "grow up" and "settle down" into a monogamous lifestyle. So what's wrong with having adventures? Can we have adventures and still raise children, buy houses and develop our careers? You bet we can. Sluts qualify for mortgages just like everybody else. We tend to like our lives complicated, with lots of stuff going on to keep us interested and engaged.

We hate boredom. We are people who are greedy to experience all that life has to offer, and also generous in sharing what we have to offer to others. We are the good times had by all.

SEXUAL DIVERSITY

This book is written for everybody — straight, gay, bi, male, female, transsexual, pansexual and more. In writing to include everyone, we will use some language in a way that may be new to some readers. We have deliberately mixed up our use of male and female pronouns, because we're sick of words like "s/he" and we can't quite wrap our traditionally grammatical minds around the singular pronoun "they." We encourage you to change pronouns to fit your own situations and relationships: our intention is to celebrate sexual diversity wherever we find it.

YOUR AUTHORS

Between us, we represent a fairly large slice of the pie that is sexual diversity. Dossie has identified first as heterosexual, then as bi, and most recently as lesbian for the last sixteen years: no matter what she thought she was doing, she has always been a slut. She committed to an open sexual lifestyle twenty-seven years ago and has spent about half of that time living single. She is currently partnered to a fabulous woman, and makes her living as a therapist specializing in relationship issues and alternative sexualities. Catherine lived as a teenaged slut in college, but then essayed monogamy in a traditional heterosexual marriage for well over a decade. Since then, she has come out as bisexual; she currently lives in a committed open relationship with a male partner, and maintains a loving live-apart relationship with a girlfriend. She writes books (under this name and her other pseudonym "Lady Green"), and runs the publishing company that brought you this book. We are both mothers of grown or near-grown children. Both of us also maintain intimate and sexual connections with one another and with extensive extended families of lovers and friends.

Here are a couple of scenes from our lives, one a moment of pain, one a moment of pleasure, which we chose to help you understand why and how we live the way we do.

Dossie: *My lover is late coming home. I hope she is all right — this morning she left in tears. Last night we both cried until very late — my eyes still burn. I hope she will not be too angry with me, or then again, her anger might be easier to bear than if she just hurts. Last night I thought my heart would break from feeling her pain.*

And it's my fault, my choice, my responsibility. I am asking my lover to go through the fire for reasons most of the rest of the world consider frivolous if not downright reprehensible — I am asking my lover to suffer because I hate monogamy.

I have hated monogamy for twenty-seven years, since I left my daughter's violent father, fighting my way out the door, bruised and pregnant, promising anything, promising I would call my parents for money, lying. After I escaped Joe he sent me suicide threats, and threatened murder — one time he almost found us and set fires around the house he thought we were still in.

Joe was very possessive. Initially I found this attractive, proof positive that he really cared about me...

My lover is back. She brought me a flower. She still doesn't want a hug. She feels her house has been invaded by alien energy. I was very careful to clean up, all is very tidy, dinner is ready, appeasement and placation, I'll do anything not to feel so horrid. My lover doesn't want to go to a movie, she isn't hungry, she guesses she'll take a shower.

Joe was very possessive. I was perfectly faithful. He would beat me, screaming imprecations, "You slut!" when another man looked at me. After I left, I decided he was right — I am a slut, I want to be a slut, I will never promise monogamy again. After all, why would anybody care who I fucked? I will never be a piece of property again, no matter how valuable that property is considered.

Joe made a feminist of me. A feminist slut. This was in San Francisco in 1969, so I decided to invent a new lifestyle. I was sick of being valued by my success at decorating some man's arm, and I was perfectly terrible at being Susie Homemaker. I like winning chess games and talking philosophy. I often talk more than I listen. I very very much wanted to be free to simply enjoy sex, for whatever reason with whoever came my way that I liked. I also needed to find my strength and my independence from knights in shining armor, so I vowed to remain single for five years in order to figure out who I am when I am running my own life. I made a life creed out of looseness.

My lover is still petting the dog. Goddess, the vibes are horrible. Why did I insist on doing this? I'm in no way perishing from unfulfilled lust. I actually wasn't even particularly horny, or salivating for Catherine and Catherine only. We have always had a sexual relationship, my co-author and me, that is part of how we write books, and how we are the dearest of friends. We have been patiently waiting to resume that relationship when my newfound and most beloved partner was ready. My lover has already conquered the terrors of group sex — tomorrow we will have another couple over for dinner and my birthday spanking, which she herself arranged with no egging on from me. She never was embarrassed at orgies, much to her own amazement. Within the last year she has had more new sexual experiences than possibly she had in the previous forty-eight years, and taken to it all like a duck to water. Except this.

Except her lover having a date with one other person. She has trouble accepting me having sex that doesn't include her, has trouble feeling left out, has trouble that we are doing it in our home this time, not neutral territory. Maybe this was a mistake. Maybe I make a lot of mistakes.

She still won't come near me. The air is heavy with pain, her voice thick with anger — how could I hurt her like this? Goddess, I hate this.

The family had welcomed her with open arms and everything else. When I decided to create my new way twenty-five years ago, I figured that I would never again take my security from my relationship, particularly not from the sexual exclusivity of my relationship. Joe had cheated on me, I knew that, it didn't even bother me very much. I sort of expected it. I resented those cultural values that said that my sense of security and self-worth were contingent on the status of whatever man I managed to attract to me, as if I had no status of my own. So I vowed to discover a security in myself, the stable ground of my very own being, something to do, I thought, with self-respect and self-acceptance. But what about other people? What about support? What about love?

San Francisco in 1969 was still very much in the communal era, so I figured I would get my support from my extended family, my kinship network that consisted of everybody that I was connected to, through friendship, communal living, coparenting, and/or sex. And it worked. Being openly open, and loudly unavailable for partnering, created a new kind of environment. I introduced my lovers to each other and lots of them liked each other. People had new experiences. Male lovers met female lovers, dykes met queers, many people made many connections. A couple of other single mothers (there were a lot of us after the Summer of Love) joined with me — we called our household Liberated Ladies at Large.

There is still a tendency for loose lovers to form kinship networks from their sexual connections, and customs, even sort of a culture, has begun to emerge. And so it is customary, in my brand new culture, for one's lovers to welcome a new lover as, not competition, but an addition to the community. And a very concrete addition at that —

I remember the first time I partnered with an equally sexually gregarious woman, and we hastened to ensure that each of us had the opportunity to have sex with each of the other's lovers: welcome to the family.

My lover is ready to talk now. She is pissed. She is seriously pissed. She resents me for every miserable terrified thought she has had today, she is furious that I would subject her to the unprotected experience of her own feelings, and that's not what she said, that's my interpretation. And that's not what I said either — this was no time to get uppity about clean boundaries and the importance of owning your own feelings. I listened. This time I listened, without interrupting, trying only to let her know that I love her, I feel her pain, I am here for her — this is very painful. She is furious with me and I am not giving myself permission to defend myself, and I hurt.

This story has no tidy ending — we talked for hours, or maybe I listened, and I heard how difficult it was for her, how she felt invaded, how she felt her home was not safe, how she feared that my other lover would not like her, how she felt attacked by her and me both, how very much she feared I was abandoning her. We came to no pat little answers that make good stories for books — we just poured out anguish, and went to sleep exhausted. We woke up the next morning feeling better, but still not over it — the issue resurfaced occasionally for the next couple of days. The birthday party helped, a subsequent date with Catherine and her girlfriend and my lover and me helped, although it was difficult.

My lover and I are still in love, and still working on it. We are committed to this relationship, and to working through our differences with compassion for each other and ourselves. I am from time to time terrified that she will leave me, just because I hate monogamy.

Catherine: *I'm in the bedroom right now. My life partner is in the bathroom, showering another woman's juices off his skin as he gets ready to go teach a class tonight. And how, as the shrinks used to say, does that make me feel?*

Well, I wish he'd get out of the shower and turn off the TV because I'm trying to concentrate. And I'm glad that my housemate/lover is downstairs talking to the other woman so that I don't have to go be sociable when I'd rather work. But aside from that, I'm feeling fine, enjoying a quiet moment in which to write, and wondering idly about what to serve my teenaged kids for dinner.

For most people, I guess, this would be unthinkable. I'm supposed to be feeling rejected and insecure, awash in rage and jealousy. If I were really good at this, I'd throw stuff at him, cry, threaten to leave him. So what's wrong with me?

Whatever it is, it's been "wrong" for a long time. The first night I spent with my husband-to-be took place because my best friend, who had come to drive me to a doctor's appointment the next day, was spending the night with my current boyfriend — with my wholehearted approval. During my young adulthood, my friends and I shared lovers as casually and generously as we shared munchies.

And then, somehow, I hit my early 20s and began, without much thought or volition, to turn into a "normal" person. We got married in his parents' church. We had a couple of kids. We bought a house, then a bigger one. We spent long hours at work. I can't remember ever even discussing whether or not we wanted to be monogamous — we just were.

Ten years later, I awoke to find myself a slut stranded in suburbia.

I started questioning some assumptions that we'd taken for granted. What if I got together with others but didn't have intercourse with them? What if I brought home a lover for both of us to share? No, no, no. He didn't feel comfortable with any of those options. I felt more and more trapped. He felt more and more exploited. Finally, with sadness and a sense of inevitability, we parted (mostly) friends.

Suddenly, the world was my candy store. I discovered rapidly that a woman who is interested in sex and open to many sexual experiences, but explicitly not interested in marriage, tends to become extremely popular extremely fast. I had my first female lover, my first three-way relationship. Rather quickly, I settled into a great *circle of "fuck buddies" — people I warmly liked, who I could call for a movie or a meal or a fuck or a conversation. I remember telling a recently divorced colleague — a woman of greater conventional beauty, wealth and desirability than I — that since my breakup I'd never spent a weekend night alone except by choice. She, miserable in her husband-hunting struggles, couldn't believe it. And at the time, I didn't have the words to explain to her how attractive happy, guilt-free, noncommittal sex could make a person.*

Into the midst of this comfortable menagerie fell my new partner. We were passionately in love almost from our first meeting, yet it never even occurred to us to discuss the possibility of monogamy: both of us "defaulted" to sluthood as easily as my ex and I had "defaulted" to monogamy a decade and a half before. I tell people that we were both dating others at the time we met, and simply forgot to stop. (He had never been monogamous in his life and had no intention of starting, and I'd had enough monogamy to last me several lifetimes.)

He met all the people I'd been having sex with; some he got along with, some he didn't, but he never asked me to change my behavior toward any of them. I met his lovers too, and wound up having sex with a few of them myself.

That was almost seven years ago. We've had lovers who have passed out of one of our lives only to become close friends of the other; lovers who have become so close that they've joined our household; lovers who have helped us publish our books, raise our kids, understand our lives, get our rocks off. Separately and together, we've had casual fuck buddy-hoods, intimate loving friendships, intense romantic crushes. So far — and I cross my fingers as I write this — it's all working out.

When I meet people who tell me that they are monogamous because other relationship styles are "too hard," I feel puzzled. I've done monogamy and I've done sluthood, and there's no question in my mind which one is harder for me.

Meanwhile, a little while ago my partner popped out of the shower all clean and glowing. (Yes, the TV's off, and I decided on baked beans and hot dogs for dinner.) I asked him, "So, did you have a good time?" He grinned and nodded. "And did she have a good time?" He grinned wider and nodded more emphatically. And that was that. We kissed goodbye, said "I love you," and he went off to work.

Whatever's wrong with me, I hope it never gets cured.

CHAPTER 2. VALUES AND ETHICS

VALUES: DENIAL VS. FULFILLMENT

Dossie's bachelor's thesis was entitled "Sex Is Nice And Pleasure Is Good For You." That idea is as radical now, in the '90s, as it was back in the '70s when Dossie first wrote it.

Our culture positively worships self-denial — those who unapologetically satisfy their desires, whether they be for food, recreation or sex, are vilified as immature, disgusting, even sinful. While we'll leave it to other authors to speak against anorexia and workaholism, we can certainly say that we see the path of sex-negativism and living in sexual deprivation as a harmful one. Self-loathing, hatred of one's own body and sexuality, fear and guilt over one's own sexual urges are the outcome.

We see ourselves surrounded by the "walking wounded" — by people who have been deeply, if not irrevocably, injured by fear, shame and hatred of their own sexual selves. We believe that happy connected sex is the cure for these wounds, that it is is important, possibly even essential, to most people's sense of self-worth, to their belief that life is good. We have never met anyone who had low self-esteem at the moment of orgasm.

DOES SEX NEED A "REASON"?

If you walk up to a randomly selected individual and propose that sex is nice and pleasure is good for you, you will probably hear a lot of spluttering, argument and "yahbuts" — AIDS, unwanted pregnancies, rape, the Madison Avenue commercialization of sexual desire, and so on. None of which change the core idea.

There is nothing in the world so terrific that it can't be abused if you're determined to do so: familial connections can be violated, sexual desire can be manipulated. Even chocolate can be abused. That doesn't change the basic wonderfulness of any of these things: the danger lies in the motivation of the abuser, not the nature of the item.

Sex gets a bad rap from our anhedonic culture, whose Puritan roots have led to a deep distrust of pleasure for its own sake. That distrust often expresses itself in concerns like those expressed by our mythical person on the street above. If there were no such thing as sexually transmitted disease, if nobody got pregnant unless they wanted to, if all sex were consensual and pleasurable, how would the world feel about it then? How would *you* feel?

If you look deep inside yourself, we bet you can find bits and pieces of sex-negativism, often hiding behind judgmental words like "promiscuous," "hedonistic," "decadent" and "nonproductive." (The two of us are about as slutty as you can get, and *we're* certainly not immune to this sort of cultural programming.)

Even people who consider themselves sex-positive and sexually liberated often fall into a different trap — the trap of rationalizing sex. Releasing physical tension, relieving menstrual symptoms, maintaining mental health, preventing prostate problems, making babies, cementing relationships and so on are all admirable goals, and wonderful side benefits of sex. But they are not what sex is *for*. Sex is for pleasure, a complete and worthwhile goal in and of itself. People have sex because it feels very good, and then they feel good about themselves. The worthiness of pleasure is one of the core values of ethical sluthood.

ETHICS

We are ethical people, ethical sluts. It is very important to us to treat people well and not hurt anyone. Our ethics come from our own sense of rightness, and from the empathy and love we hold for those around us. It is not okay with us to hurt another person because then we hurt too, and we don't feel good about ourselves.

Ethical slutdom is a challenging path: we don't have a poly-amorous Miss Manners telling us how to do our thing courteously and respectfully, so we have to make it up as we go along. However, we're sure you've figured out by now that to us, being a slut doesn't mean simply doing whatever you want, whenever you want, with whomever you want.

So in this slightly disorienting world of sluthood, in which everything your mom, your minister, your spouse and your television ever told you is probably wrong, how do you find your ethical center?

Most of our criteria for ethics are quite pragmatic. Is anyone being harmed? Is there any way to avoid causing that harm? Are there any risks? Is everybody involved aware of those risks and doing what can be done to minimize them?

And, on the positive side: How much fun is it? What is everybody learning from it? Is it helping someone to grow? Is it helping make the world a better place?

First and foremost, ethical sluts value *consent*. When we use this word — and we will, often, throughout this book — we mean "an active collaboration for the benefit, well-being and pleasure of all persons concerned." If someone is being coerced, bullied, blackmailed, manipulated, lied to or ignored, what is happening is not consensual. And sex which is not consensual is not ethical — period.

Ethical sluts are *honest* — with ourselves and others. We take time with ourselves, to figure out our own emotions and motivations, and to untangle them for greater clarity when necessary. Then we openly share that information with those who need it. We do our best not to let our fears and bashfulness be an obstacle to our honesty — we trust that our partners will go on respecting and loving us, warts and all.

Ethical sluts also *recognize the ramifications* of our sexual choices. We see that our emotions, our upbringing and the standards of our culture often conflict with our sexual desires. And we make a conscious commitment to supporting ourselves and our partners as we deal with those conflicts, honestly and honorably.

We do not allow our sexual choices to have an unnecessary impact on those who have not consented to participate. We are *respectful* of others' feelings, and when we aren't sure how someone feels, we ask.

Ethical sluts recognize the difference between things they can and should control, and things they can't. While we sometimes may feel jealous or territorial, we *own those feelings* — doing our best not to blame or control, but asking for the support we need to help ourselves feel safe and cared for.

All of this can be hard, but your authors are here to help. We wrote this book to help you become an ethical slut.

Sex and Relationships

Our monogamy-centrist culture tends to assume that the purpose and ultimate goal of all relationships — and, for that matter, all sex — is lifetime pair-bonding, and that any relationship which falls short of that goal has failed. We disagree.

We think sexual pleasure can certainly contribute to love, commitment, and long-term stability, if that's what you want. But those are hardly the only good reasons for having sex. We believe in valuing relationships for what makes them valuable, a seeming tautology which is wiser than it sounds.

A relationship may be valuable simply because it affords sexual pleasure to those involved; there is nothing wrong with sex for sex's sake. Or it might involve sex as a pathway to other lovely things — intimacy, connection, companionship, even romantic love — which in no way obviates the basic goodness of the pleasurable sex.

A sexual relationship may last for an hour or two. It's still a relationship; the participants have related to one another, as sex partners, companions and/or lovers, for the duration of their interaction. Longevity is not a good criterion by which to judge the success or failure of a relationship: Edna St. Vincent Millay wrote:

> *After all, my erstwhile dear,*
> *My no longer cherished,*
> *Need we say it wasn't love*
> *Just because it perished?*[1]

One-night stands can be intense, life-enhancing and fulfilling; so can lifetime love affairs. While ethical sluts may choose to have some kinds of relationships and not others, we believe that all relationships have the potential to teach us, move us, and above all give us pleasure.

Our friend Jaymes says, "I believe that every person you connect with on this planet has some sort of a message to give you. If you cut yourself off from whatever kind of relationship wants to form with that person, you're failing to pick up your messages."

Or, to put it another way, Dossie remembers an interview with a young flower child back in 1967 who made the most succinct statement of ethical sluthood we've ever seen: "We believe it's okay to have sex with anybody you love... and we believe in loving everybody!"

See there? You don't need a lot of "thou shalt nots" to be an ethical person. Honesty, empathy, foresight, integrity, intelligence and respect will do just fine.

CHAPTER 3. PARADIGMS, OLD AND NEW

We're sure you don't need us to tell you that the world does not, for the most part, honor sluthood, or think well of those who are sexually explorative. In this chapter we'll discuss some of the ideas and assumptions that have helped make so many sluts feel bad about themselves. While you read them, you might like think about what all these judgments about sluts tell us about our culture.

"PROMISCUOUS"

This means we enjoy too many sexual partners. This word alone has possibly created more unhappy sluts than any other. (We've also been called "indiscriminate" in our sexuality, which we resent: we can *always* tell our lovers apart.)

We do not believe that there is such a thing as too much sex, except perhaps on certain happy occasions when our options exceed our abilities, nor do we believe that the ethics we are talking about here have anything to do with moderation or abstinence. Kinsey once defined a "nymphomaniac" as "someone who has more sex than you."[2]

Is having less sex somehow more virtuous than having more? We think not. We measure the ethics of a good slut not by the number of his partners, but by the respect and care with which he treats them.

"Amoral"

Our culture also tells us that sluts are evil, uncaring, amoral and destructive — Jezebel, Casanova, Don Juan. Watch out! The mythological evil slut is grasping and manipulative, seeking to steal something — virtue, money, self-esteem — from his partners. In some ways, this archetype is based on the idea that sex is a commodity, a coin you trade for something else — stability, children, a wedding ring — and that any other transaction constitutes being cheated and betrayed. (Once when Dossie was recovering from a botched abortion a friendly nurse tried to comfort her by saying, "I know, honey, they all promise to marry you." Dossie managed to keep a straight face — the nurse was friendly and supportive, and it seemed cruel to inform her that she wouldn't have dreamed of marrying the unethical slut who by this time was conspicuous only by his cowardly absence.)

We have rarely observed any Jezebels or Casanovas in our community, but perhaps it is not very satisfying for a thief to steal what is freely given. We do not worry about being robbed of our sexual value by the people we share pleasure with.

"Sinful"

Some people base their sense of ethics on what God, or their church, or their parents, or their culture, considers okay or not okay. They believe that being good consists of obedience to laws set down by a power greater than themselves. Dossie remembers explaining to some family friends that she had left the church she was raised in because she didn't believe a just God would punish her aunt for getting a (much justified) divorce. The family friends were pretty conservative people, and of an older generation. One of them asked, "Well, if you don't believe God will punish you, why don't you just go around murdering people?" Dossie explained that she doesn't murder people because her internal sense of ethics, her empathy with others, and her desire to feel good about herself, all tell her that to harm another person would be a terrible thing for her to do.

To believe that God doesn't like sex is like believing that God doesn't like you: we all wind up carrying a secret shame for our own perfectly natural sexual desires and fulfillments. We prefer the beliefs of a woman we met who is a devoted churchgoer. She told us that when she was about five years old, she discovered the joys of masturbation in the back seat of the family car, tucked under a warm blanket on a long trip. It felt so wonderful that she concluded that the existence of her clitoris was proof positive that God loved her.

"PATHOLOGICAL"

In the late 19th Century, with the advent of psychological studies of sexual behavior, Krafft-Ebing and Freud attempted to preach more tolerance by theorizing that sluts are not bad, but sick, suffering from psychopathology that is not their fault, since their neurosis derives from having their sexuality warped by their parents during their toilet training. So, theoretically, we should no longer burn sluts at the stake, but send them to mental hospitals to be cured of repression in an atmosphere that permits no sexual expression whatsoever.

During your authors' childhood and adolescence in the early '60s, it was still common practice to certify and incarcerate adolescents for "treatment" of the "illness" of being sexual, especially if they were gay or lesbian, or female and in danger of damaging their market value as virgins. Heterosexual men were virtually never pathologized and incarcerated to prevent them from being sexual before they were eighteen.

Consider the concept of nymphomania, a disease never attributed to men. It is woman, enjoying sex with no one in control except herself, who is considered dangerous and sick. Dossie notes that in three decades of being a sex radical, she has observed only one incidence of a person driven by such indiscriminate and constant sexual need that it constituted a destructive force in her life, who in Dossie's opinion matched the criteria for nymphomania. But she has clients in her therapy practice who describe themselves as nymphomaniacs if they masturbate every day.

"ADDICTED"

More recently we hear about sex addicts and avoidance of intimacy. Sex addiction is usually defined as the substitution of sex for nourishment of other needs, like to allay anxiety or bolster sagging self-esteem. Such people may have compulsive needs to "score," to succeed sexually with a large number of partners, or to get validation for their sexual attractiveness over and over, as if they need constant reassurance because at the core they do not see themselves as attractive and lovable.

Sex *can* be misused as a substitute for connection, emotional relationship or a solid sense of internal security based on knowing your own worth. Some sexual abuse survivors become what is called "sexualized" in a childhood where the closest approximation to adult attention, validation and affection they had was molestation. Such survivors may need to expand their options and learn other ways to get their needs met. On the other hand, "sex addict" seems to be the latest incarnation of cultural judgment about sluts: a good friend of Catherine's once told her, quite seriously, that the reason Catherine was so contented was that she was a sex addict who had managed to find a way to make a lifestyle out of her addiction.

If you are working on any of these issues, we suggest that you put some thought into how you would like your sexuality to be different in the future. Some twelve-step groups and therapists may try to tell you that anything but the most conservative of sexual behaviors is wrong, or unhealthy, or "into your addiction"; we encourage you to trust your own beliefs and find yourself a more supportive environment. If your goal is monogamy, that's fine, and if your goal is to stop seeking sex in the place of friendship, or any other behavior pattern that you wish to resculpt, that's fine too. We do not believe that successfully recovering sex addicts have to be monogamous unless they want to be.

"EASY"

Is there, we wonder, some virtue in being difficult?

Myths About Sluts

One of the challenges facing the ethical slut is our culture's insistence that, simply because "everybody knows" something, it must inevitably be true. A lot of these cultural paradigms have become almost invisible; people take them as much for granted as the air they breathe or the ground they walk on. Questioning what "everybody knows" is sometimes difficult and disorienting, but we have found it to be rewarding — questioning is the first step toward creating a *new* paradigm, one that may fit you better.

We urge you to regard with great skepticism any sentence that begins "Everybody knows that..." or "Common sense tells us that..." or "It's common knowledge that...." Often, these phrases are signposts for cultural belief systems which may be antisexual, monogamy-centrist and/or codependent.

Cultural belief systems can be *very* deeply rooted in literature, law and archetype, which means that shaking them from your own personal ethos can be difficult. But the first step in exploring them is, of course, recognizing them.

Here, then, are some of the pervasive myths that we have heard all our lives, and have come to understand are most often untrue and destructive to our relationships and our lives.

MYTH #1: LONG–TERM MONOGAMOUS RELATIONSHIPS ARE THE ONLY *REAL* RELATIONSHIPS.

Lifetime monogamy as an ideal is a relatively new concept in human history, and makes us unique among primates. There is nothing that can be achieved within a long-term monogamous relationship that cannot be achieved without one — business partnership, deep romantic attachment, stable parenting, personal growth, and care and companionship during the aging process are all well within the abilities of the slut.

People who believe this myth may feel that something is wrong with them if they aren't in a committed twosome — if they prefer to remain "free agents," if they discover themselves loving more than one person at a time, if they have tried one or more traditional relationships that didn't work out. Instead of questioning the myth, they question themselves. Such people often have a very romantic view of couplehood — that Mr. or Ms. Right will automatically solve all their problems, fill all the gaps, make their lives complete.

One friend of ours points out that if something goes wrong in a monogamous marriage, nobody takes that as evidence against the practicality of monogamy — but if something goes awry in an open relationship, many folks instantly take that as proof that non-monogamy doesn't work.

A subset of this myth is the belief that if you're really in love, you will automatically lose all interest in others, and thus, if you're having sexual or romantic feelings toward anyone but your partner, you're not really in love. This myth has cost many people a great deal of happiness through the centuries, yet is untrue to the point of absurdity; a ring around the finger does not cause a nerve block to the genitals. Even happily monogamous couples recognize the realities of outside sexual and romantic desire: if Jimmy Carter could lust in his heart, so can you.

MYTH #2: SEXUAL DESIRE IS A DESTRUCTIVE FORCE.

This one goes all the way back to the Garden of Eden, and leads to a lot of crazy-making double standards. In this worldview, men are hopelessly sexually voracious and predatory, and women are supposed to control and civilize them by being pure, asexual and withholding. Thus the openly sexual woman destroys civilization.

Many people also believe that unashamed sexual desire, particularly desire for many people, destroys the family — yet we suspect that far more families have been destroyed by bitter divorces over adultery than have ever been disturbed by ethical consensual nonmonogamy.

MYTH #3: LOVING SOMEONE MAKES IT OK TO CONTROL HIS BEHAVIOR.

This kind of territorial reasoning is designed, we guess, to make people feel secure — but we don't believe that anybody has the right, much less the obligation, to control the behavior of another functioning adult. Being treated according to this myth doesn't make us feel secure, it makes us feel furious. The old "awww, she's jealous — she must really care about me" reasoning, or the scene in which the girl falls in love with the boy when he punches out a rival suitor, are symptomatic of a very disturbed set of personal boundaries which can lead to a great deal of unhappiness.

This myth also leads to the belief, so often promulgated in Hollywood films and popular literature, that fucking someone else is something you do *to* your partner, not *for* yourself — and is, moreover, the very worst thing you can do to someone. (For many years, adultery was the only legally acceptable grounds for divorce, leaving those who had unfortunately married batterers or drunks in a very difficult position.) People who believe this often believe that nonmonogamy must be nonconsensual, in order to protect the sensibilities of the "betrayed" partner.

MYTH #4. JEALOUSY IS INEVITABLE AND IMPOSSIBLE TO OVERCOME.

Jealousy is, without a doubt, a very common experience in our culture — so much so that a person who doesn't experience jealousy is looked at as a bit odd, or in denial. But the fact is that a situation which would cause intense jealousy for one person can be no big deal for another. Some people get jealous when their honey takes a sip out of someone else's Coke, others happily watch their beloved wave bye-bye for a month of amorous sporting with a friend at the far end of the country. Jealousy is common, but far from inevitable.

Some people also believe that jealousy is such a shattering emotion that they have no choice but to succumb to it. On the contrary, we have found that jealousy is an emotion like any other: it feels bad (sometimes *very* bad), but it is not intolerable; sometimes the best thing to do with jealousy is simply to allow yourself to feel it. We have also found that many of the thinking patterns which lead to jealousy can be unlearned, and that unlearning them is often a useful process. Later in this book, we will discuss jealousy in much greater detail.

MYTH #5: OUTSIDE INVOLVEMENTS REDUCE INTIMACY IN THE PRIMARY RELATIONSHIP AND IMPEDE PROBLEM—SOLVING.

Most marriage counselors are taught that when a member of an otherwise happily married couple has an "affair," this must be a symptom of unresolved conflict or unfulfilled needs that should be dealt with in the primary relationship. Sometimes this is true, and equally often it is not. The problem is that this myth leaves no room for the possibility of growthful and constructive open sexual lifestyles. It is cruel and insensitive to interpret an affair as a symptom of sickness in the relationship, as it leaves the "cheated-on" partner — who may already be feeling insecure — to wonder what is wrong with him. Meanwhile, the "cheating" partner gets told that she is only "acting out" to get back at her primary partner, and she really doesn't want, need or even like her lover.

Many people have sex outside their primary relationships for reasons that have nothing to do with any inadequacy in their partner or in the relationship. Perhaps this outside relationship allows a particular kind of intimacy that the primary partner doesn't even want, such as fetish behavior or particular sexual activities, and thus constitutes a resolution of an otherwise insoluble conflict. Or perhaps it meets other needs — such as a need for uncomplicated physical sex without the trappings of relationship, or for sex with someone of a gender other than one's partner's, or for sex at a time when it is otherwise not available (during travel or a partner's illness, for example). Or it may simply be a natural extension of an emotional and/or physical attraction to someone besides the primary partner.

An outside involvement does not in any way have to subtract from the intimacy you share with your partner unless you let it. And we sincerely hope you won't.

MYTH #6: "SWEPT AWAY BY LOVE."

Hollywood tells us that "love means never having to say you're sorry," and we, fools that we are, believe it. This myth has it that if you're really in love with someone, you never have to argue, disagree, communicate, negotiate or do any other kind of work. It also tells us that love means we automatically get turned on by our beloved, and that we never have to do anything to deliberately kindle passion. Those who believe this myth may find themselves feeling that their love has failed every time they need to schedule a discussion or to have a courteous (or not-so-courteous) disagreement. They may also believe that any sexual behavior that doesn't fit their criteria for "normal" sex — from fantasies to vibrators — is "artificial," and indicates that something is lacking in the quality of their love.

What We Believe

So we just spent a whole section telling you about all the concepts and mythologies the world may believe about sluts. Now, we'll tell you our side of the story — the way we look at our lives and the lives of the people we know.

YOU ARE ALREADY WHOLE

Jane Austen wrote, "It is a truth universally acknowledged that a single man in possession of a good fortune must be in want of a wife."[3] While we think Jane probably had her tongue firmly planted in her cheek, a great many people do believe that to be single is to be somehow incomplete, and that they need to find their "other half." A lot of the myths we mentioned in the previous section are based in that belief.

We believe, on the other hand, that the fundamental sexual unit is one person; adding more people to that unit may be intimate, fun and companionable but does not complete anybody. The only thing in this world that you can control is yourself — your own reactions, desires and behaviors. Thus, a fundamental step in ethical sluthood is to bring your locus of control into yourself — to recognize the difference between your "stuff" and other people's. When you do this, you become able to complete yourself. That's why we call this "integrity."

You may notice that the parts of this book are based in that idea: in Part I, we talk about the ideas and concepts you need to grasp within yourself; in Part II, we talk about interactions with other sluts; and in Part III, we discuss interactions with the world. (In Part IV, we cover the fun stuff that didn't fit in anywhere else.) Similarly, throughout the book, every time we introduce a new idea or concept, we will start by discussing how it works for the individual — you need to understand these concepts, and how they apply to you, before you can begin communicating your needs and ideas to the other people in your life. When you have built a satisfying relationship with yourself, then you have something of great worth to share with others.

STARVATION ECONOMIES

Many people believe, explicitly or implicitly, that romantic love, intimacy and connection are finite capabilities of which there is never enough to go around, and that if you give some to one person, you must be taking some away from another.

We call this belief a "starvation economy"; we'll talk much more about it in Part II. Many of us learn to think this way in childhood, from parents who have little intimacy or attention for us, so we learn that there is only a limited amount of love in the world and we have to fight for whatever we get — often in cutthroat competition with our brothers and sisters.

People who operate from starvation economies can become very possessive about the people, things and ideas that matter to them. They are working from a paradigm that anything they get comes from a small pool of not-enough, and must thus be taken from someone else — and, similarly, that anything anyone else gets must be taken from them.

It is important to distinguish between starvation economies and real-world limits. Time, for example, is a real-world limit; even the most dedicated slut has only twenty-four hours every day. Love is not a real-world limit: the mother of nine children can love each of them as much as the mother of an only child.

Our belief is that the human capacity for sex and love and intimacy is far greater than most people think — possibly infinite — and that having a lot of satisfying connections simply makes it possible for you to have a lot more. Imagine what it would feel like to live in an abundance of sex and love, to feel that you had all of both that you could possibly want, free of any feelings of deprivation or neediness. Imagine how strong you would feel if you got to exercise your "love muscles" that much, and how much love you would have to give!

Openness can be the solution, not the problem

Is sexual adventurousness simply a way to avoid intimacy? Not usually, in our experience.

While it is certainly possible to use your outside relationships in order to avoid problems or intimacy in your primary relationship, we do not agree that this pattern is inevitable or even common. Many people, in fact, find that their outside relationships can *increase* their intimacy with their primary partner by reducing the pressures on that relationship, and by giving them a safe place to express issues that may have them feeling "stuck" in the primary relationship.

These are our beliefs. You get to have beliefs of your own. What matters to us is not that you agree with us, but that you question the prevailing paradigm and decide for yourself what you believe. Thousands and thousands of ethical sluts are proving every day that the old "everybody knows" myths don't *have* to be true.

We encourage you to explore your own realities and create your own ethos — one that spurs you onward in your evolution, that supports you as you grow, and that reflects your pride and happiness in your newfound relationships.

CHAPTER 4. THE LANGUAGE IN THIS BOOK

TOWARD A SEX-POSITIVE LANGUAGE

Most of the language available for us to talk about sex has built-in value judgments, just like the word "slut" — the legacy of our sex-negative history. Without language, how are we to communicate with each other, share our thoughts and feelings? Without language, we can hardly even *think* about sex. So efforts have been made to develop a language with which to talk dirty... whoops, pardon us: to talk about sex in a clean and positive way. Here are some terms that we use:

• **Sex.** You thought you already knew what this meant, didn't you? Well, we're not sure that *we* do. We have had long intense intimate conversations that felt deeply sexual to us. On the other hand, we have had intercourse that didn't feel terribly sexual.

Our best definition here is that sex is whatever the people engaging in it think it is. For some people, spanking is sex. For others, wearing a garter belt and stockings is sex. If you and anybody else involved feel sexual when you eat ice-cream sundaes together, that's sex — for you. While this may sound silly now, it's a concept that will come in handy later in this book when we discuss making agreements about our sexual behaviors.

- **Sex-negative.** Sex is dangerous. Sexual desire is wrong. Female sexuality is destructive and evil. Male sexuality is predatory and uncontrollable. It is the task of every civilized human being to confine sexuality within very narrow limits. Sex is the work of the devil. God hates sex. Got the picture?

- **Sex-positive.** The belief that sex is a healthy force in our lives. This phrase was created by sex educators at the National Sex Forum in the late '60s. It describes a person or group which maintains an optimistic, open-minded, nonjudgmental attitude toward all forms of consensual sexuality.

- **Nonjudgmental.** An attitude which is free of irrational or unjustifiable moralizing. "Nonjudgmental" does not mean all-accepting; it means being willing to judge an activity or relationship on the basis of how well it works for the participants and not on some external standard of absolute rightness or wrongness. Sometimes it means getting bigger than your judgments, just for a minute, so you can take a good look at them.

- **Nonmonogamy.** We don't like this term, because it implies that monogamy is the norm and that any other way of relating is somehow a deviation from that norm.

- **Monogamy-centrist.** The prevailing attitude in most cultures today: the belief that monogamy is the only natural and moral sexual pattern, or the normal or highest form of human relationship (often coupled with the terms "long-term" or "lifelong"). This concept is so taken for granted that we usually don't even notice or question it — your authors had to invent a term to describe it.

- **Couple-centrist.** Another widely prevailing attitude: the belief that the couple is the fundamental human sexual unit, and that any other relationship structure must eventually evolve toward couplehood, and that you are incomplete without a partner, your "other half." We believe that couples, and other groupings based on sex and love, are made up of individuals who complete themselves, then come together to share.

- **Polyamory.** A word which has gained a great deal of currency in recent years. We like it because, unlike "nonmonogamy," it does not assume monogamy as a norm. On the other hand, its meaning is still a bit vague: some feel that polyamory includes all forms of sexual relationships other than monogamy, others restrict it to committed love relationships (thereby excluding swinging, casual sexual contact and other forms of intimacy).

- **Polyfidelity.** A subset of polyamory, in which more than two people, possibly two or more couples, form a sexually exclusive group. Sometimes used as a safer sex strategy.

- **Polymorphous perverse.** Polymorphous means "having many forms," and perverse means "abnormal" or "wrong." Freud used this expression to describe the sexual behavior of children under five years of age, who tend to be very explorative with no regard whatsoever for boundaries or conventional limits until taught otherwise by adults[4]: if it feels good, young kids will do it. Modern sexual explorers sometimes use this term to describe themselves, perverting Freud's intention to a more modern reading of pursuing sexual pleasure in any and all forms, without regard to defining constructs like straight, gay, vanilla, or outrageous.

• **Open relationships.** A term that describes relationships in which sexual and romantic connections are not restricted to the two members of the couple. We like to use it a bit more loosely for any relationship in which the people involved have some degree of freedom to fuck and/or love people outside the relationship, so that an eight-person group marriage may still be either "open" or "closed."

• **Free love.** The only reason we're not using this phrase more often in this book is because we're afraid we'll sound like the aging hippies we are. In Catherine's adolescence and Dossie's young adulthood, this was the phrase used joyously by many (and disgustedly by many more) to describe a lifestyle in which sex, affection and love were shared as a means of interpersonal connection as well as an idealistic sociopolitical statement. It saddens us that the values of our culture have turned away from this ideal, which we still believe to be both achievable and desirable for many people.

• **Sexual freedom.** A term from the '60s that still has a lot of juice in it. One of the earliest groups to attempt to live out many of the ideas in this book was called the Sexual Freedom League. Since we like sex and we like freedom, we like this phrase.

Sexual freedom implies casting off the chains of our sex-negative programming and returning to innocence, manifested as a Garden of Eden of sex and love. Back in the '60s, we believed we could do that just by declaring ourselves to be free. We quickly learned that freedom doesn't come that easy: it requires effort, work.

Luckily for all of us, sexual misery is a powerful motivator, a very sharp stick that prods us donkeys up the road, into doing that hard work of coming to grips with our fears about sex. And lucky for us, we eventually can get to the carrot of sexual delight and fulfillment, and isn't that carrot sweet!

CHAPTER 5. ANCESTORS & ANTECEDENTS

Sluts come in all the various forms and styles that humans come in: men and women in all cultures, from all parts of the world, of all religions and lifestyles, rich and poor, with formal and informal education.

Most of us today live in communities of non-sluts, with only occasional or limited contact with other people who share our values: some groups hold conferences and conventions to mitigate the isolation and expand their intimate circles. Other sluts drop out of mainstream culture to some extent or another to live in communities composed of people whose sexuality is like their own. San Francisco's Castro District is a good example of a modern urban "ghetto" for sexual minorities.

A slut living in mainstream, monogamy-centrist culture in the '90s can learn a great deal from studying other cultures, other places, and other times: you're *not* the only one in the world who has ever tried this, it *can* work, others have done it without harming themselves, their lovers, their kids — without, in fact, doing anything except enjoying themselves.

Pioneering sexual subcultures with extensive documented and undocumented histories include communities of gay men and of lesbian women, transgender groups, bisexuals, the leather communities, the swing communities, and some spiritually defined subcultures of pagans, modern primitives and radical faeries.

Even if you don't belong to any of these sexually oriented communities, it's worth taking a look at them for what they can teach us about our own options as they develop ways of being sexual, ways of communicating about being sexual, and social and family structures that are alternative to sex-negative traditions in America.

Dossie's favorite dance club in 1970 was a remarkable miniculture of polymorphous perversity. She remembers:

> *The Omni, short for omnisexual, was a small North Beach bar whose patrons were men and women, straight, gay, lesbian, bisexual and often transgendered. The sexual values were very open, from hippie free-love freaks to sex industry professionals, and most of us came there to dance like wild women and cruise like crazy. However, thanks to the large transgender faction, there was no way of pigeonholing the person you were cruising into your categories of desire. You might dance with someone you found very attractive, and not know if they were chromosomally male or female. It's difficult to get attached to preferences like lesbian or straight when you don't know the gender of the person you are flirting with.*
>
> *This may sound crazy, but the results were surprising: I patronized the Omni because it was the safest environment available to me. Because there was no way to make assumptions, people had to treat each other with respect. No one could assume what kind of interaction might interest the object of their attention, so there was nothing to do but ask. And if you were, as I was, a young woman in your twenties, to be approached with respect*

*was a most welcome relief from straight social
environments where it was customary for men to prove
their manhood by coming on too strong, evidently in the
belief that women who cruise in single bars have
problems with virginal shyness and don't mean "no"
when they say it. The Omni provided my first experiences
with true respect.*

Since we see some of the problems in attaining a free and open
expression of our own individual sexuality as having to do with living in
a sex-role-bound culture, we have found it useful to learn from people
who have shifted the boundaries of what it means to be male or female,
or to love someone male or female. Thinking about these different ways
of living and loving can help us as we consider whether we want to
change anything about how we go about living as men and women.

LESBIAN WOMEN

In the lesbian community we get to look at what happens in a world
consisting almost entirely of women. The first thing we can see is an
intensification of the mainstream values that teach us that men focus
their energy out into the world while women specialize in relationships,
families and emotional nurturance. The lesbian community tends to be
relationship-centered, and has both weaknesses and strengths in the
way that women find their primary relationship to be the most important
thing in their lives. For women, relationship can get confused with their
sense of identity, especially since our culture in its most traditional form
hardly allows women any sense of identity at all.

Dossie had a psychiatrist, admittedly some years ago, who
advised her that she would not be happy and mentally healthy until

she gave up her artistic and intellectual pursuits and (an exact quote) "submerged her identity in a relationship." Submerge identity — sounds like psychological suicide, right? But many women today act as if they would lose their entire sense of themselves if they lose their relationship, so the most common relationship sequence, as we see it magnified in the lesbian community, is the form of nonmonogamy known as serial monogamy. Often the connection to the partner of the future precedes the breakup with the partner of the past, with accompanying drama that presumably feels safer than the vast empty unknown terrifying identity void of being a woman living as a single human being.

Younger lesbians are questioning these traditions, and one of the ways they are questioning is in investigating nonmonogamy as a way to form less insular relationships. Lesbian free love is characterized by a lot of serious thoughtfulness and attention to consensuality, and thus to tremendous openness about processing feelings, an area in which the women's community excels.

Another thing we have learned from our sisters is new ways of dealing with developing a woman's role as sexual initiator. In heterosexual culture, men have been assigned the "job" of initiator, and men are trained to be sexually aggressive, sometimes to a fault. In the world of women who relate sexually to other women, it rapidly becomes apparent that if we all see ourselves as Sleeping Beauties waiting for Princess Charming to come along and wake us up, we also might get to wait a hundred years. Or else we need to learn to do something new — to meet the eye, touch the shoulder, move in a little too close, or just plain blurt out "I think you're really attractive and I would like to leap into bed with you right now or at any other mutually agreeable time."

Women's style of coming on — when shyness doesn't get in the way — tends to be forthright, with respect for consent, and is unlikely to be intrusive or pushy, as many women have had a little too much experience with being violated to want to go down that road. Women have strong concerns about safety, and so tend to move slowly, announce their intentions and be very careful about consensuality. They may be shy in the seductive stages, and bolder once welcome has been secured. Women tend to want explicit permission, and for each specific act, so their communication could serve as an excellent role model for negotiated consensuality.

We would like to draw your attention to another difference about sex between women that we all can learn from. A sexual encounter between two women rarely involves the expectation of simultaneous orgasm, as many people believe penis-vagina intercourse should, so women have become experts at taking turns. Lesbians are also the world-class experts on sensuality and outercourse, those wonderful forms of sexuality that do not rely on penile penetration. When penetration is desired, the focus is on what works for the recipient: we have yet to meet a dildo that got hung up on its own needs. For those of you, female or male, who haven't considered these options, think of all the fun you could have with never a worry about pregnancy and sexually transmitted diseases!

GAY MEN

The gay male community in its own way reflects some of the traditional images of male sexuality in intensified form. While some gay men are more interested in long-term relationships and settling down, other gay men have set records as world-class sluts. The gay baths are the ultimate role model of friendly group sex environments, and easy sexual connection for its own sake.

Dossie learned her group sex etiquette from gay men, and is glad she did. We both, in fact, have always identified strongly with gay men: Dossie sees herself as a drag queen trapped in a woman's body, and Catherine got her earliest sense of her own sexual possibilities when she learned about gay male communities. This may not really be too surprising, since the gay male community has always modeled sluttery for the rest of us to admire and, perhaps, emulate.

Gay men do not generally try to get consent from each other by manipulation and pressuring: connection is mostly commonly made by a gentle approach, meeting a gentle response, and no need to ask three times. Gay men give each other a lot of credit for being able to say no, and for meaning it when they say it. This makes coming on very simple, since you are never trying to sneak up on anybody and you are not required to be subtle. It is always okay to ask as long as it is okay for the other person to say no. This straightforward and admirably simple approach to consensuality cannot be recommended too highly.

Men in general have had less reason to fear sexual violation than their sisters. (Although it is true, and terrible, that boys do get molested and men do get raped, we think that perhaps men have more confidence than women in their power to protect themselves.) Men also tend to get a lot of cultural support for being sexual. So although the forbiddenness of homosexuality may give many gay men a lot of questions about being okay, or having something wrong with them, or other forms of internalized homophobia, this is most often not reflected in sexual dysfunction. Gay men as a group are really good at exploring, and finding out what feels good to them.

And it is gay men who have established most of our understanding of safer sex. In the face of the AIDS epidemic, where many people might have retreated into sex-negativism, the gay community is to be commended for continuing to celebrate a newly liberated sexuality, with due respect for safety.

TRANSGENDER

Transgendered people form a variety of communities, all of which are of interest to anyone who is interested in transcending their gender-role programming. Dossie, in the early years of her feminism, found friends among male-to-female transsexuals who were wonderful role models for how to be female, indeed often ultra-feminine, and still be assertive and powerful.

What we can all learn from transgendered people is that gender is malleable. We learn about how some behaviors and emotional states may be hormone-related from people who take hormones to express male or female gender. People who have lived parts of their lives in both gender modes, physiologically and culturally, have a great deal to teach us about what changes according to hormones, and what does not, and what gender characteristics remain a matter of choice no matter what your endocrine system says.

Transsexuals can also tell us a lot about how differently other people treat you when they see you as a man, or as a woman. Perforce, transgendered people become experts at living in a very hostile world. No other sexual minority is more likely to suffer direct physical oppression in the form of queer bashing. It takes a strong minded person to stand up to our culture's rigidity about "real men" and "real women." It was mostly transgendered people, butch women and drag queens, who rebelled against police brutality in the famous Stonewall riots of 1969 that initiated the Gay Liberation movement. Transgendered people can teach us a lot about the determination to be free.

BISEXUALS

Often stigmatized as "gays unwilling to relinquish heterosexual privilege" or "hets taking a walk on the wild side," bisexuals have recently begun developing their own forceful voice and their own communities.

Looking at the theory and practice of bisexual lifestyles may enable us to explore our assumptions about the nature of sexual and romantic attractions and behaviors. Some folks have had sex only with members of one gender, but know that they have within themselves the ability to connect erotically or emotionally with both genders, and thus consider themselves bisexual — while others may be actively having sex with the gender opposite their usual choice, and still consider themselves heterosexual or gay. Some bisexuals prefer one type of interaction with men and another with women, while others consider themselves "gender-blind." Some can be sexual with either sex but romantic with only one, or vice versa. And so on, through all the spectrums of bisexual attractions and choices.

Catherine's path toward her current identity as a bisexual has been a confusing one: it was nearly a decade after she began having sex with women before she began to feel comfortable using the term to describe herself.

I felt turned off by the trendiness of "bisexual chic,"
and under some pressure to claim an identity that didn't
feel right to me. And at the same time, I was hearing
some genuinely cruel judgments from both heterosexuals

*and homosexuals about bis, and that anger was scary to
encounter.*

*Add to that the difficulty I was having sorting out my
own feelings — I knew my feelings toward women were
different than those toward men, and I wasn't sure what
that meant — and things just got very confusing. As a
result, it wasn't until I knew for sure that I was capable
of having both sexual and romantic feelings toward both
men and women — and until I felt strong enough to claim
the identity in the face of all those negative judgments —
that I finally began calling myself "bisexual."*

The increasing visibility of bisexuality has led to some challenges
to traditional definitions of sexual identity. Specifically, we are having
to look at the fact that our sexual attractions may say one thing about us,
while our sexual behaviors say another, and our sexual identity says yet
a third. Questions like these are eating away at some of the traditional
boundaries we place around sexual identity — much to the dismay of
purists of all orientations. Your authors, sluts that we are, enjoy this kind
of fluidity, and appreciate the opportunity to play as we like with
whomever looks good to us without relinquishing our fundamental sexual
identities.

SWINGERS

In bygone decades, nonmonogamous heterosexual interactions got called
"wife-swapping" — a term with a built-in sexist bias which we find
offensive. Today, heterosexuals seeking no-strings sex outside a primary
relationship often seek out the swing community. These groups are well
worth looking at for what they have to teach us about how heterosexual

men and women can interact outside the confines of the "shoulds" of mainstream, monogamous culture.

Swinging is a broad term that gets used to define a wide variety of interactions, ranging from long-term two-couple sexual pairings through the wildest of Saturday-night puppy-pile orgies. Swingers are primarily heterosexual: female bisexuality is relatively common in some swing groups, while male bisexuality is rare and frowned upon in most. They are most often coupled, and are often more mainstream in their politics, lifestyles and personal values than other kinds of sluts. Some swing communities confine themselves explicitly to sexual interactions and discourage emotional connections outside primary couples, while others encourage all forms of romantic and sexual partnering.

Swinging has offered many a heterosexual woman her first opportunity to explore greedy and guilt-free sexuality — in fact, we often hear of women who attend their first swing party very reluctantly, their second one hesitantly, and their subsequent ones avidly. We also like the sophistication with which many swing communities have evolved patterns of symbols and behavior to communicate sexual interest without intrusiveness (one local swing club has a fascinating code of opening doors and windows to communicate, variously, "Keep away," "Look but don't touch," or "Come on in and join us").

Sex workers

How about if we stop stereotyping sex workers? They're really not all desperate drug addicts, debased women, or whatever you might have learned about them on TV or in the tabloids. Many of our dearest friends work in the sex industry, doing essential and positive work healing the wounds inflicted by our sex-negative culture. These men and women have a great deal to teach us about boundaries, limit-setting, communication, sexual negotiation, and ways to achieve growth, connection and fulfillment outside a traditional monogamous relationship. Do not imagine that connections between sex workers and clients are necessarily cold, impersonal, or degrading, or that only losers frequent prostitutes. We know of client/prostitute relationships that have been a source of tremendous connection, warmth and affection for both parties, and that have lasted many years. Practitioners of "the world's oldest profession" offer all of us the wisdom of the ages about understanding, accepting and fulfilling our desires: these are the real sex experts.

SACRED SLUTS

Finally a word about sexually explorative lifestyles in spiritual communities. Celibacy is not the only sexual practice of the spiritually inclined. Early examples of religious communities based on nonmonogamy included the Mormon church, the Oneida community, the practice of maithuna and karezza in Tantric Yoga, and the temple whores of the early Meditaerranean Goddess worshipers. Current sexually active spiritual communities include some pagan groups and radical faeries, who come together for festivals and gatherings, and celebrate ancient sexual rites such as Beltane, or make up their own that are appropriate to current lifestyles, like the open sexuality of Faery gatherings, or the underlying eroticism of ritual.

These practitioners understand that sex is connected to the spiritual. We have said before that sex is spiritual. "Every orgasm is a spiritual experience. Think of a moment of perfect wholeness, of yourself in perfect unity, of expanded awareness that transcends the split between mind and body and integrates all the parts of you in ecstatic consciousness.... When you bring spiritual awareness to your sexual practice, you can become directly conscious of — connected to — that divinity that always flows through you.... For us, sex is already an opportunity to see god."[5]

What Can You Learn?

If thinking about all this makes you kind of nervous, we are not surprised. What you are being exposed to is how threatened you feel when limits are very different from what you are used to — those customary boundaries we take for granted and believe apply to all social and sexual situations. There are no universally accepted boundaries of gender or attraction among consenting adults, and the limits of sexual exploration are not handed down on stone tablets by some higher authority.

When you look at people who meet your standards of happiness and success without buying into the world's standards of lifetime heterosexual monogamous pair-bonding, you begin to see how such things can be possible for you too — even if these people aren't doing it the same way you want to. Recognizing other sexual cultures offers an opportunity to become aware of where your own buttons are, especially when you think about keeping them buttoned up around a lot of people whose sexuality may be different from yours. Listen to your fears: they have a lot to teach you about yourself.

Think of Dossie's old dance club, The Omni. Not knowing what's what can feel scary — but think of it as a chance to scrap all your preconceptions and start from scratch. It's only by recognizing all the possibilities out there that you can truly choose the ones that work for you. Then you can be free to figure where you want the boundaries to be in your life, what your personal limits are, and if you ever want to expand them.

This is a great opportunity as well as a serious responsibility. Once you have established your own limits, you are free to explore beyond your wildest dreams.

CHAPTER 6. SLUT SKILLS

Great sluts are made, not born. The skills you need to keep yourself and your partners happy and growing can be developed through a combination of conscious effort and frequent practice. There are certain thought processes you can try, and skills you can learn, that will help start your adventure on the right foot and keep it on track.

Self-examination, in our opinion, is always a good idea — and for we who are journeying without a map, having a clear picture of the *internal* landscape becomes essential. Here's an interesting question to ask yourself: What do you expect from this way of living your life? What rewards can you foresee that will compensate you for doing the hard work of learning to be secure in a world of shifting relationships? Some people who have already made the journey cite benefits like sexual variety, less dependence on a single relationship, or a sense of belonging to a network of friends, lovers and partners. Some of the people we interviewed said things like this:

"I get relief from pressure — I don't have to fulfill every single thing my partner needs or wants, which means I don't have to try to be somebody I'm not."

"People have different ways of knowing and understanding things, so intimacy with various people expands my appreciation of the universe."

"I can have hot erotic experiences without genital sex, and without compromising my emotional monogamy."

"My lifestyle gives me personal freedom, independence and responsibility in a way that being an exclusive couple does not."

"I don't believe that the human male is designed to be monogamous. Monogamy goes against my instincts."

"I never feel that the grass might be greener on the other side of the fence — I've been there."

"Outside partners are an infusion of sexual juice into my primary relationship."

As you read this book, particularly some of our interviews with successful sluts, you may discover special benefits for you. What are your reasons for choosing this path?

Alas, many people begin to explore open relationships because their partner is pushing them into it, or because all their friends are doing it and they don't want to seem prudish. We ask that you get clear within yourself that you're doing this for *you* — because it excites you, because it offers opportunities for learning and growth and fun, because you want to. Make no mistake, this can be a rocky road... and if you're navigating it for the wrong reasons, resentment can easily poison the very relationships you set out to save.

Sexual change can be a path of reprogramming yourself, with the joyous feeling of abundant sex and love as the carrot, and the fear of deprivation, boredom or self-loathing as the stick. Since we don't believe that the urge toward monogamy is innate, we think you must have learned your negative sexual feelings and your insecurities *somewhere*

— from your parents, from your past lovers, from our culture — and, thus, you can unlearn them. Becoming aware of those feelings, and changing your reactions to them, can be difficult... but what a feeling of power and triumph when you succeed!

Earning Your Slut Merit Badge

The people we know who succeed at ethical slutdom usually have a set of skills that help them forge their pathway cleanly, honestly, and with a minimum of unnecessary pain. Here are some of the ones we've noticed.

COMMUNICATION

Learning to talk clearly, and listen effectively, are critical skills. A good technique for listening is to hear what your partner has to say, and let him know you heard by telling him what you think he just said. Use this clarification technique *before* you respond with your own thoughts and feelings. In this way, you make sure you have clear understanding before you go on with your discussion. Similarly, if you're the one talking, it's not fair to expect your partner to read your mind — take the time and effort to be as clear and thorough in your explanation as you can, and be sure to include information about the emotions you're feeling as well as the facts involved.

If your communications often seem to go awry, it might be a good idea to spend some time and effort learning better communication skills: many adult education facilities offer communication classes of various kinds, and you can check the Resource Guide for further reading.

EMOTIONAL HONESTY

Being able to ask for and receive reassurance and support is extremely important. Catherine's partner occasionally requests, when she is off to a joyously anticipated date with one of her other lovers, "Just tell me I don't have anything to worry about." It feels very good to know that he's willing to ask for reassurance when he needs it, and that he trusts her to tell the truth about her feelings. If you imagine what would happen if he were feeling insecure and *didn't* ask for reassurance (grumble, chew fingernails, lie awake thinking bad thoughts, etc., etc.), you can see why it's so important to get your needs met up front.

We have all been afraid to ask, we have all failed to ask, we have all been irked with our lovers when they didn't read our minds, we have all thought "I shouldn't *have* to ask." So let's honor the courage it takes to ask for support, to share vulnerable feelings — let's pat ourselves on the back when we do the things that scare us, and then let's do them some more.

Affection

Similarly, it's vital to be able to *give* reassurance and support — both in response to a request, and on your own. If you can't tell your lover that you love him, or give him a heartfelt compliment, or tell him what you think is so wonderful about him, it may be optimistic to assume that he'll be able to remain secure enough to accommodate your other relationships. Our friend Carol notes, "If you're already starved for attention, no wonder an open relationship feels like a problem!" We recommend lots of hugging, touching, verbal affection, sincere flattery, little "love ya" gifts, and whatever else helps both of you feel secure and connected.

Faithfulness

This may seem like an odd word to read in this context — but even the most outrageous of sluts can be, in the words of Cole Porter, "always true to you, darlin', in my fashion." Our friend Richard says, "A lot of people describe having sex with only one person as 'being faithful.' It seems to me that faithfulness has very little to do with who you have sex with." Faithfulness is about honoring your commitments and respecting your friends and lovers, about caring for their well-being as well as your own.

If you have a primary relationship, it can be very important to reinforce its primary-ness. Many people in primary relationships have certain activities that they keep only for their partners — particular sexual behaviors, sleep-overs, terms of affection or whatever. The same may also be true of other, non-primary relationships. Without the security blanket of monogamy, it becomes very important to help your partner feel more secure by demonstrating how much you care for her — and if this means that once in a while you choose to miss your favorite TV show, or even give up a hot date, because she's sick, or having a life crisis, or just feeling lonely and blue, we think that is well worth doing.

LIMIT-SETTING

To be a happy slut, you need to know how — and when — to say "no." Having a clear sense of your own limits, and respecting those limits, can keep you feeling good about yourself and prevent those morning-after blues. Some limits may be about sexual behaviors: Would you have sex with a gender other than the one you usually do? Would you try a kind of sex you think is kinky? Some limits might be about relationship styles, such as frequency of contact or intensity of connection. We also encourage you to think about ethical dilemmas and how you'd react to them. Would you, for example, be a lover to a coupled individual whose partner didn't know about your involvement? Would you lie to a lover? Fake an orgasm?

And then there's the most important limit of all: "I don't want to." "No, thank you." "I don't feel like sex right now." Even if it's your birthday. Even if you're supposed to want to. Even if you haven't for a long time. Just because it's true.

PLANNING

Successful sluts know that relationships don't just happen — they take work, planning, and commitment. Few of us have so much time on our hands that we can simply have conversations, sex, recreation, family time, or even fights whenever we feel like it — mundane reality has a way of getting in the way of such important stuff. And yes, we do think fighting is important and necessary — we'll talk more about the hows and whys in the chapter on "Conflict" in Part II. If scheduling a fight seems a little bit absurd, just imagine the results of letting the tension build for several days because you *haven't* made time to argue.

Get yourself an appointment calendar, and use it (Catherine used to schedule sex with her husband, whose name began with F, with the cryptic note "F.F." — just in case a co-worker should glance into her Day Runner). And once you've made the commitment to spend time together doing any of these things, keep it — we know you're busy, but postponing important relationship work to attend to business does not speak well of the significance you give your relationships, does it?

KNOW YOURSELF

And know your programming. As we have said before, we are all carrying around a lot of garbage in our minds about sex and gender. No one can grow up in our culture and escape picking up puritanical and inaccurate ideas about sex. Some of these beliefs are buried so deep they can drive our behavior unconsciously, without our knowing it, and cause a great deal of pain and confusion to ourselves and the people we love. All too often, in the name of these beliefs, we oppress other people, and ourselves.

These deeply held beliefs are the roots of sexism and sex-negativism, and to be a radical slut you are going to have to uproot them. To truly know yourself is to live on a constant journey of self-exploration, to learn about yourself from reading, therapy, and, most of all, talking incessantly with others who are traveling on similar paths. This is hard work, but well worth it because this is the way you become free to choose how you want to live and love, own your life, and become truly the author of your experience.

OWN YOUR FEELINGS

A basic precept of intimate communication is that each person owns her own feelings. No one "makes" me feel jealous, or insecure — the person who makes me feel that way is me. This belief is not as easy as it sounds. When I feel rotten, it can be hard to accept the responsibility for how I feel: wouldn't this be easier if it were your fault? Then maybe you could fix it, and if you can't, well then maybe I can go ballistic and vent a little steam, burning you up in the process.

The problem is that when I blame you for how I feel, I disempower myself to accept myself and work toward feeling better. If this is your fault, you must be in control, right? So I can't do anything but sit here and moan.

On the other hand, when I own my feelings, I have lots of choices, I can tell you how I feel, I can choose whether or not I want to act on

Dos and Don'ts of Ethical Sluttery

DO ARRANGE YOUR OWN TRANSPORTATION WITHOUT DEPRIVING YOUR PARTNER OF THE CAR.

DON'T GET YOUR LOVER'S PUBIC HAIRS IN THE ALBOLENE.

DON'T FUCK LOUDLY AND ENTHUSIASTICALLY WITHIN YOUR LOVER'S HEARING.

DON'T WANDER OFF WITH YOUR LOVER, LEAVING YOUR PARTNER TO MAKE CONVERSATION WITH YOUR LOVER'S SPOUSE.

DO REFRAIN FROM FUCKING THE GUESTS UNTIL YOUR LOVER IS FINISHED COOKING AND SERVING DINNER.

DON'T TELL YOUR LOVER MORE THAN YOUR LOVER WANTS TO KNOW.

DON'T REGARD "IT WAS SUCH A GOOD FUCK" AS AN ADEQUATE EXCUSE FOR COMING HOME LATE WITHOUT CALLING.

DON'T EXPECT NECESSARILY TO LIKE YOUR PARTNER'S LOVERS.

DON'T EXPECT THY PARTNER TO BE INTENSELY HORNY FOR YOU RIGHT AFTER HAVING SEX WITH SOMEONE ELSE.

DO GET THE TRICK TOWELS INTO THE HAMPER BEFORE YOUR LOVER GETS HOME.

these feelings (no more "the devil made me do it!"), I can learn how to understand myself better, I can comfort myself, or ask you to comfort me. Owning your feelings is basic to understanding the boundaries of where I end and you begin, and the perfect first step toward self-acceptance and self-love.

Go easy on yourself

As prepared as you are, as centered as you are, as stable as you are, you *are* going to trip over problems you never anticipated — we guarantee it.

Perhaps the most important step in dealing with problems is to recognize that they will happen, and that it's OK that they do. You'll make mistakes. You'll encounter beliefs, myths and "buttons" you never knew you had. There will be times when you'll feel pretty awful.

Can we tell you how to avoid feeling bad? Nope. But we think you'd forgive a friend or lover who misunderstood or made a mistake, and we hope you'll grant yourself the same amnesty. (As Morticia Addams says: "Don't beat yourself up, Gomez; that's *my* job.") Knowing, loving and respecting yourself is an absolute prerequisite to knowing, loving and respecting someone else. Cut yourself some slack.

A friend of ours, when he makes a mistake, says, philosophically, "Oh well — AFOG." That stands, he says, for Another Fucking Opportunity for Growth. Learning from one's mistakes isn't fun, but it's better than not learning at all, right?

Tell the truth

Throughout your experience — as you feel pain, ambivalence, joy — you must speak your own truth, first to yourself, then to those around you. "Stuffing" and self-deception have no place in this lifestyle: pretending that you feel great when you're in agony will not make you a better slut; it will make you bitterly unhappy, and it may make those who care about you even unhappier.

When you tell the truth, you discover how much you have in common with the people you care about, and put yourself in an excellent position to support yourself and each other in a life based on understanding and loving acceptance. As you dig deeper and share your discoveries, you may learn more about yourself and others than you ever knew before. Welcome that knowledge, and keep on digging for more.

CHAPTER 7. SLUTSTYLES

There are a whole lot of ways to live your sexual life, a whole lot of different ways to relate to people and form relationships and families, and no one way is better than all the others.

WHAT IS NORMAL? WHAT IS NATURAL?

Our culture teaches us that only one way of relating — long-term monogamous marriage – is the right or the best way. We are told that lifetime monogamy is "normal" and "natural," and that if we do not manage to force our desires into a single relationship we are morally deficient, and somehow going against nature. But the truth of our natures is that many of us desire sex with more than one person. So why does our culture require monogamy?

Historically, requirements for sexual fidelity to one partner are linked with sex-negative attitudes and attempts to control sexuality in the interest of society. "Control" is the key word here — in particular the control of reproduction in the interest of primogeniture or other dynastic goals.

When our culture was agrarian, and infant mortality common, having lots of children to work the farm in your old age was a good survival tactic, and mixing the gene pool not such a bad idea either. When we look back on marriage in the agrarian world, we see that much of its purpose was dynastic, to ensure the orderly succession of property and production so that the family and the village had enough food, houses to live in and general stability to maximize physical safety and well-being. In these villages, and in many parts of the world today, the extended family was what was important, the network of kinship that ensured a large basis of mutual physical and emotional support. The extended family still exists to some degree in America today, often in cultures recently transplanted from other countries, or as a basic support system among economically vulnerable urban or rural populations.

The prudishness that characterizes much of our cultural heritage is a relatively new thing — in the last century, only relatively wealthy people had master bedrooms; most people had their sex in the same room with their children and their parents. In warmer climes, you had your sex outdoors. In one African culture, proper etiquette taught to young people prescribes that if you come across a couple copulating in the bushes, the polite thing to do is to quietly sit on your heel and rock back and forth till you have an orgasm too. Wouldn't that be a different way to grow up!

The control of reproduction became increasingly important as our culture became more urban — indeed, we see an increasing focus on controlling sex since the Industrial Revolution in Europe. It was at this time, in the late 18th century, that we began to hear that masturbation was bad for you, that this most innocent of sexual outlets was dangerous to society: 19th century childrearing manuals show devices to prevent babies from touching their genitals in their sleep. So our very interest in sex, not even acted on with another, became our shameful secret.

Wilhelm Reich put forth an interesting theory in his lectures to young Communists in Germany in 1936, during the rise of Hitler. Reich theorized that without the suppression of sexuality and the imposition of anti-sexual morality, you could not have an authoritarian government, because people would be free from shame, and would trust their own sense of right and wrong. Such people are unlikely to march to war against their wishes, and we would like to think they would be unlikely to agree to operate the death camps too.[6] It is interesting to think that if we were raised without shame and guilt about our desires, we might be freer people in many ways.

The nuclear family, which consists of parents and children relatively isolated from sisters and cousins and aunts, is an artifact of the modern middle class. Children no longer work on the farm or in the family business; they are raised almost like pets. Modern marriages, no longer essential for survival, have become luxuries whose primary purpose is to fulfill our needs for sex, intimacy, and emotional connection. We are convinced that the increase in divorce reflects the simple economic reality that most of us can today afford to leave relationships that we no longer find satisfying.

And still the puritans, perhaps not yet ready to deal with the frightening prospect of truly free sexual and romantic choice, attempt to enforce the nuclear family and monogamous marriage by teaching sexual shame.

We believe that the current set of prescribed "oughtabes," and any other set, are cultural artifacts. We believe that Nature is wondrously diverse, offering us infinite possibilities. We would like to live in a culture that respects the choices made by sluts as highly as we respect the couple celebrating their fiftieth anniversary. (And, come to think of it, what makes us assume that such a couple is monogamous anyway?)

We are paving new roads across new territory. We have no culturally approved scripts for open sexual lifestyles; we pretty much need to write our own. To write your own script requires a lot of effort, and a lot of honesty, and is the kind of hard work that brings many rewards. You may find the right way for you, and three years from now decide you want to live a different way — and that's fine too. You write the script, you get to make the choices, and you get to change your mind, too.

Endless Possibilities

The possibilities for rewarding and constructive slut lifestyles are indeed endless, so we can't cover them all. We will describe some of the lifestyles that have worked for some people. Whether or not any of these scenarios fit for you, we hope that they will offer you some ideas about where to start your exploration, or perhaps the validation of knowing that there are others like you out there.

Remember that there are many kinds and degrees of intimacy, as many as there are people. We have seen a lot of people get confused, and have been confused ourselves, when we try to force a relationship to satisfy some fantasy or ideal that does not fit that particular relationship. When we meet someone we like and feel sexy about, this is not an indication that that person will fit precisely into the empty space in our lives. And it will not work to make a point-by-point evaluation of a potential playmate, scoring her according to how closely she matches up to our fantasy of the ideal partner. Putting our own needs and fantasies foremost gets in the way of actually meeting another person, and enjoying the wonderful surprises involved in getting to know who that person is.

Each relationship seeks its own level. You might get along fabulously with your friend, and have great sex with colossal intimacy... yet discover from experience that this works when you get together about once a month. Maybe when you try to spend a week together you get irritated, or bored, or otherwise very unhappy with the situation. If you allow this relationship to work the way it works, you could go on meeting once a month for ten years and be perfectly content.

One of the wonderful advantages of being a slut is that you get to have different kinds of relationships, instead of having to choose just one. When we are looking for a life partner, for example, we want a lot of compatibility: similar values, intellectual and esthetic interests in common, good sex, likes to eat the same food. We can connect with a much wider range of people as soon as we stop auditioning them for a together-forever role. You don't have to force anyone into a mold that doesn't fit: all you have to do is enjoy how you *do* fit together, and let go of the rest.

FRIENDLY SEX

Nothing challenges culturally imposed boundaries for intimacy more than opening up the potential to share sex with friends. Catherine had lunch a while ago with Mary, one of the few friends remaining from her previous life as a monogamous married woman. At one point Mary remarked, "Hey, I guess I'm about the only straight friend you have left, huh?" "Yup," Catherine agreed. "In fact, you're the only friend I've never had sex with."

In singles culture, we can observe the "Land of One-Night Stands," in which you go home with a pick-up and share some hot sex, then the next morning you look at each other and decide if the relationship has life-partner potential. If not, you leave, with much embarrassment, and the unspoken rule is that you will never be comfortable with that person again, as they have been weighed in the balance and found wanting. We have no scripts for sexual intimacy in the middle, in the area between complete stranger and total commitment.

How do you learn to share intimacy without falling in love? We would propose that we do love our friends, and particularly those we share sex with: these individuals are our family, often more permanent in our lives than marriages. With practice, we can develop an intimacy based on warmth and mutual respect, much freer than desperation, neediness, or the blind insanity of falling in love. That's why the relationships between fuck-buddies are so immensely valuable. When we acknowledge the love and respect and appreciation that we do share with lovers we would never marry, sexual friendships can become, not only possible, but preferred. So while you're worrying that your sexual desire could cost you your best friend, the more experienced slut could be wondering — like Catherine — why you are the only friend he has never fucked.

Each relationship seeks its own level, or will if you let it. Like water, you and whatever person has caught your fancy can flow together as long as you let it happen in the way that is fitting to you both.

There are infinitely many ways in which people can come together, so here we will list only a few of the patterns that we have observed work well for some of the people we have known. All these get modified by your sexual preferences: monosexual, bisexual, transgender, S/M. Here we are talking about what are essentially the family structures of sluts.

CELIBACY

Traditionally, celibacy has offered a way for people to focus on intellectual or spiritual concerns, without the distraction of fleshly lusts. If you're on a religious quest, or working on your doctoral dissertation, or undergoing a major life change, celibacy — short-term or long-term — may offer a valid means of narrowing your focus for a while.

Similarly, people for whom sex or relationships have been problematic may choose a period of celibacy as a pathway toward self-examination: "What kind of person am I when I'm by myself?" (Dossie was celibate for this reason for five months after she left her abusive partner.)

Some people are celibate, but not by choice: people who are incarcerated, ill or disabled, geographically isolated, socially unskilled, or underage may have trouble finding partners for consensual sex. Others are celibate simply because they do not, for whatever reason, feel like being sociable or sexual for a while.

We do not see "celibate slut" as in any way a contradiction in terms. Unless your spiritual quest dictates otherwise, a period of celibacy can offer a wonderful "honeymoon for one": a period that you can spend in lengthy and luxurious exploration of your own fantasies, turn-ons and physical reactions to various stimuli. Masturbation can and should be a sexual art equal to partnered sex in its possibilities and complexity, a genuine and honorable manifestation of self-love. And celibacy can become a triumphant celebration of your relationship with yourself.

SINGLEHOOD

For some sluts, being single may be a temporary condition between partners, or a recommended period of healing from a recent breakup, or a chosen lifestyle for the long term. Being single is a good way to get to know who you are when you are not trying to fit as the other half of somebody else; learning to live with yourself and enjoy it gives you a lot to share with a partner when you choose to have one. Dossie has spent about half of her adult life unpartnered, generating a kinship network from playing the field, raising her daughter in a very supportive community of mutually loving and sexual men and women.

Single people can play the field in a variety of ways. One distinguishing dimension is how separate you keep your lovers. We may go to great lengths to protect our lovers and ourselves from experiencing any jealousy, to the extent that we often fail to learn how to deal with jealous feelings because we have given ourselves no opportunities to try — but more about this later. We promise we will help you with jealousy in its own chapter.

So one form of sluttery for the single involves multiple partners who have no interaction, indeed no information about each other. This avoids complications at the cost of limiting certain kinds of intimacy, such as opportunities for mutual support and the development of community.

Another way is to introduce your lovers to each other, perhaps over Sunday brunch. This may sound wild, or impossible, or like a script for disaster, but don't knock it if you ain't tried it. Your lovers have a lot in common, to wit you and whatever attracted you to them, and they may very well like each other: Catherine used to have a marvelously giggly biweekly lunch date with her partner's lover, who lived near her workplace. Indeed, you could go into this situation fearing that your lovers would hate each other, and come out wondering about your own jealousy if your lovers like each other a little better than you bargained for — Catherine stayed friends and occasional lovers with her partner's lover long after his sexual relationship with her had ended.

Introducing your lovers helps prevent one of the scariest aspects of jealousy, which is the part where you imagine that your lover's other lover is taller, thinner, smarter, sexier and in all ways preferable to funky old you. When you meet that other person, or when your lovers meet each other, they meet real people, warts and all, and so may wind up feeling safer. (Believe us, no flesh and blood human is scarier than your own imagination.) This also solves the annual problem about who you spend your birthday with: once they know each other, they can conspire to surprise you with a big party.

Introducing your lovers to each other also makes possible the development of a community, or an extended family of people who are intimately connected through sexual and personal bonds. As more people connect to each other in a variety of ways, including sexual, networks form, and something like families evolve. Then the situation of introducing your lovers can become obsolete, as they may already know each other.

For the single person, becoming lover to one member of a couple requires that you, as the single person, respect their relationship and be courteous and supportive to your lover's primary partner. It also requires that your lover's partner be courteous and supportive to you. Avoid falling into the trap that you are automatically the co-respondent, the seducer, the home-wrecker, the thief of love when someone who is partnered is attracted to you, or you to them. You are no more the villain than anyone else in this transaction. When all of you behave with respect for all of your feelings, there are no victims, and no villains.

The single person may also become lover to a couple, in any combination of genders. Relating to an established couple offers a lot of security to the single person, who can enter into an existing intimacy, and share whatever energy seems to suit, without further obligation. It is an incredible privilege, and a great treat, to be permitted to observe and enter into a couple's sexual pattern that has had the chance to evolve over time with the intense intimacy of partners. There is a great beauty in intimate sex, and the lover to a couple is in a great position to partake of it. Your authors both cherish memories of delicious moments in three-ways when, perhaps ourselves already sated, we got a quiet moment to watch our lovers make love to each other — a profoundly moving and beautiful sight.

If you are a single person in any open sexual lifestyle, it helps to pay attention to how you are getting your needs met, both sexual and emotional. A life of one-night stands can be warm and intimate if you make your lovers into your family — sharing your emotions with your partners, and expressing affection and appreciation for the delight you find in them. You can get your needs met in an infinite variety of ways. The important thing is to be aware of your needs and wants, so you can go about getting fulfilled with full consciousness. If you pretend that you have no needs, either for sex, or affection, or emotional support, you are lying to yourself, and you will wind up trying to get your needs met by indirect methods that won't work very well. People who do this often get called manipulative or passive-aggressive — terms, in our opinion, for people who have not figured out how to get their needs met in a straightforward manner. Do not commit yourself to a lifetime of hinting and hoping.

When you figure out what you want and ask for it, you'll be surprised how often the answer is "yes." Think how relieved you might feel when someone asks you for support, or a hug, or otherwise lets you know how to please her or him. Think of how competent and just plain good you feel when you can truly help another person, whether it's by offering a shoulder to cry on, or that just right stimulation that leads to the perfect orgasm. Give your friends the opportunity to feel good by fulfilling you too.

PARTNERSHIPS

There are multiple forms of open relationships for the partnered, including serial monogamy, where one's various partners are separated in time, and the ever-popular nonconsensual nonmonogamy, otherwise known as cheating. We can think of these lifestyles as "unconscious free love," but your authors feel both freer and safer when we stay aware.

It is axiomatic that open relationships work best when a couple takes care of each other and their relationship first, before they include others in their dynamic. So the slut couple needs to be willing to do the work we will describe later in this book to communicate well and to handle jealousy, insecurity and territoriality with the highest conscious-ness. Couples also need to keep their own sexual connection happy, healthy and hot.

Couples can have a secondary relationship outside of the primary, or a number of lovers that don't get ranked in any hierarchy. Relationships vary a lot in how close or distant they are, and in how much contact is involved. Some may be short-term, while others may last for years or even a lifetime; some may involve getting together twice a week, others twice a year.

Couples new to nonmonogamy tend to spend a lot of energy defining their boundaries. They usually focus more at first on what they *don't* want their partner to do — the activities that make them feel, for some reason, unsafe or downright terrified — than on their actual desires. This is, for many couples, a necessary first step out into the disorienting world of sluthood — these limits act as friendly handles to grab onto when you're feeling dizzy, scared or insecure. Our observation is that as couples become more sophisticated at operating the boundaries of their relationship, they tend to focus more on what they would enjoy, and then strategize about how they can make it safe.

One woman of our acquaintance has a lifetime lifestyle of having two primary partners, one of each gender, with her other partners and her primaries' other partners forming a huge network. Her primary relationships historically have lasted many years, through raising children and grandchildren, and her exes are still active members of their extended family. Her and her partners' abilities to extend love and unconditional support to so many people is remarkable.

In some open relationships, each partner seeks out other partners pretty much separately, often making agreements about who gets to cruise which club when, or taking care to avoid running into each other on the Internet or in the newspaper ads. They may talk about their adventures with each other, and occasionally introduce play partners to their primaries.

Others seek out a close match with another couple so they can play, either as a foursome or by switching partners, with people they have met and chosen together. Many polyamorous couples make a fine lifestyle out of seeking relationships with couples who are most like themselves, who share their values and boundaries. Such pairings of pairs can become lifelong attachments, and generate both hot sex and true family interconnectedness.

Couples, as well as singles, may enjoy group sex. Environments for orgies, party houses, sex clubs, swing houses, gay men's baths, the tubs or the glory holes, are available in many major cities in a variety of forms, and cater to all sexual preferences. We will tell you all about them in their own chapter. As part of a lifestyle, a group sex environment may constitute a safe field of exploration for a nonmonogamous couple. They can attend parties together or separately, cruise singly or as a twosome, meet each other's friends, and play with a variety of people, all the while maintaining whatever connection with each other they feel good about. In this way, sex outside of the primary relationship has a boundary of sorts, the specific environment in which it happens, and many people like it that way.

Group sex environments tend to develop their own families, people who come regularly and get to know each other, and may share other activities, like giant Thanksgiving dinners. The film "Personal Services" shows us a warm and marvelous Christmas get-together of such a family in a British house of domination.

Some people form sexually exclusive groups of couples, practicing polyfidelity in a closed but wider field of possibilities so that members can explore sexually and still have a container that will protect them from infection and provide a level of emotional commitment from all members. Some live separately, and some create group marriages of two or three or four couples who have made commitments to raise kids and buy houses, along with whatever agreements they work out about sharing sex.

More than two

People can make commtiments to each other in numbers greater than two. The level of commitment may vary, as when an existing couple makes a commitment to a third partner, or even a fourth. Relationships that add, and inevitably also subtract, members over time actually tend to form very complex structures, with new configurations of family roles that they generally invent by trial and error. Individuals in groups that come together as a threesome or foursome may find their roles within the family developing, growing and changing over time: the person who feels like "mother" of the group this year might well transition to "kid" or "Dad" over time.

Triads are probably the most common arrangement, allowing partners of one or both genders to form a family unit. Some people grow into triadic or quadratic families as they attain deepening involvement with one or more members who started as outside lovers. Others actively seek members for group marriages, to fulfill their idea of the kind of family they want to live in. We have heard of people who identify as "trisexual" because they are so strongly attuned to the idea of living and loving as part of a threesome.

Balancing triads can be challenging, as in any ménage a trois there are actually three couples, A & B, B & C, and C & A, and each of these relationships will be different. In a triad, as with the siblings of a family, all the relationships will not be at the same level at the same time. Catherine, for instance, recently participated in a lengthy Internet conversation regarding which member of a triad should ride in the back seat of the car. To get hung up on forcing these relationships to be exactly the same can leave you in the position of the small kid screaming about "How come she got the first hug?", or the biggest smile, or the hottest orgasm. We cannot emphasize enough the importance of getting beyond competitiveness to work inside yourself on accepting difference and uniqueness as a wonderful gift that increases us all.

CIRCLES AND TRIBES

Circle is a word we use for a set of connections between a group of people that actually might look more like a constellation, with some people near the hub and connected to several others, and others near the outside and connected to only one or two (and, perhaps, part of another constellation as well). These constellations may be casual, or may become actual extended families, with provisions for raising children, making a living, taking care of the sick or aging, and purchasing property.

University of Pennsylvania professor James Ramey, in his wonderful book "Intimate Friendships," documented his observations that nonmonogamy tended toward the forming of what he described as kinship networks, communities bound together by the intimacies of their sexual connections, perhaps serving the same functions as villages did in a smaller world.[7] Some of us have taking to referring to our groupings as tribes.

Circles of sexual friends are common — gay men call these friends "fuck buddies." Such circles may be open, and welcome new members, typically brought in by other members. When you are part of such a circle, new lovers of any member are potential friends and family members of your own, so the focus changes from competition and exclusivity to a sense of inclusion and welcome, often very warm indeed.

Other circles are closed, with new members welcome only by agreement with existing members. Closed circles have become more popular as a strategy for safety from HIV infection and other sexually transmitted conditions, and also to deal with alienation in an overpopulated world. In a closed circle, the notion is that you can play with anyone in the circle (all of whom have made agreements about safer sex, and are all perhaps of known HIV status) but you don't have sex with anyone outside the group. Thus you get to play around with a variety of relationships and still stay in a limited field. Such lifestyles are sometimes known as polyfidelity.

Group marriages, of any number, may be formed by a group of couples or may actually avoid dyads, focusing on everyone being an individual member of the group. Groups may also be closed or open. They may choose to celebrate the inclusion of a new member into the family with a marriage-type ceremony — Catherine recently encountered a group of three friends who were shopping together for wedding rings.

The Unethical Slut: Ways *Not* to Do It

Some people approach open sexual lifestyles as if the most important aspect is the score, and there is no referee. All's fair, right? Sport fuckers, set collectors and trophy fuckers treat their partners like prizes in a contest they have set out to win — only what happens after the prize is collected? Is it time to go after the next one?

The concept of set collectors may be new to you, but we assure you that such people exist. Dossie discovered a bunch of them when she lived in a communal San Francisco household called Liberated Ladies at Large with two other single mothers, and learned that some people's ideal of free love was to make sure they had sex with all three of the liberated sisters. Catherine once discovered that a would-be lover of hers had already had sex with her mother and her sister, and was hoping for a perfect score.

When sport-fucking means treating your partners as objects rather than as human beings, this does not meet our requirements for mutual respect. We hope you aspire to more from your sexual encounters than to score a few points in the game of love: we prefer to play for real.

Some people approach "scoring" as if all people could be ranked on a hierarchy from the most to the least desirable, and as if the way to make the most points and assure yourself of a high rank were to collect partners as high up the ladder as you could reach. People gain in rank and value in these hierarchies by being rich, thin, young, cute, wealthy and/or professional, and sometimes by owning expensive wardrobes, cars or other property. You will note that these attributes, the ones you can measure, are all about external characteristics, rather than about the kind of person this is or the warmth and depth of the connection you could make.

We do not believe that love is a game which you can win by scoring high on a hierarchy of shallow values. We know from extensive experience that a fashionable appearance is not a predictor of good loving. We avoid ranking people as better or worse than each other, and are unhappy with those who want to relate to our rank (authors get quite a few points in the "profession" category) more than our selves. Hierarchies produce victims on the top as well as the bottom, since it is just about as alienating to be approached by too many people for the wrong reasons as it is to be approached by no one at all. We know that each person is unique, and that their own individuality is far more valuable than how they look or what they own.

Some people enter into sexual encounters as though sex were a big game hunt — trying to conquer the unwilling, and unwitting, victim, as though the object of their attentions would never make a decision to share sex with the seducer unless tricked into it. Have we all seen or read "Dangerous Liaisons"? If you believe that someone else would have to be a fool to make love with you, that may be a self-fulfilling prophecy. If you believe that you can use sex to shore up your fragile self-esteem by stealing someone else's, we feel sorry for you, because this will never work to build a solid sense of self worth, and you will have to go on stealing more and more and never getting fulfilled. And we hope you play the thief of love in some other social circles than our own.

Often, someone who has a history of nonconsensual nonmonogamy gets attached to the sense of secrecy, of "getting away with something." These folks may have a very hard time adapting to the idea of consensual sluthood — they're so used to concealing their activities from their partners that they may even have built that furtive feeling into their erotic life, feeling hooked on the adrenaline rush they get from forbidden fruit. It may take a pretty substantial leap of faith, and maybe some creative fantasizing and role-playing, for such an individual to open up her hidden places and experience the greater joy that can come from knowing that nobody is getting hurt by her fun.

Don't make promises you can't keep. If you are attracted to someone who is looking for a life partnership and what you want is a light-hearted affair (or vice versa), you need to be honest about that, even if that means saying no thank you to sex until your feelings for each other are more on a par. Mistakes can easily be made. Dossie made such a mistake when she was very young and stupid:

> *I had just broken up a long term relationship, and was pretty broken up about it myself. I had gone out to the coffee shops in Greenwich Village, and saw my recent ex in earnest conversation with a cute young thing who was not me. I felt horribly betrayed, lost and worthless. Just then, a young man who had been attracted to me, and for whom I had no serious feelings, came up to speak to me. It somehow seemed appropriate to go home with him and let him soothe my ruffled feathers, but I regretted it the next day when I found myself hurting his feelings and leaving him in the lurch. To further aggravate my guilt, it turned out what my ex was doing with that sweet girl was beating his bosom about how horrible he felt about breaking up with me, and we wound up getting back together. I have always felt like I took advantage of the young man who offered me his affection, which I thoughtlessly took and then gave right back to him. It would have been kinder had I just said no.*

An older and wiser Dossie has since discovered a couple of limits of her own: she does not share sex with anyone that she's not at least potentially interested in sharing sex with again, and anything worth doing is worth waiting for till the time is right. While we all make mistakes, the hallmark of a skillful slut is to learn from them and keep going.

Which brings us to revenge fucking. It is truly nasty to arrange to have sex with one person to get back at another. To arouse one person's insecurities, jealousy and other painful feelings on purpose is dishonorable, and to use another person like a puppet in your play in this fashion is disrespectful and often downright abusive. In psychopathology, "antisocial" is defined as behaving with flagrant disregard for the rights, and we would add feelings, of others. We prefer to relate to sociable people.

What do you do when someone in your intimate circle is not playing honestly? It helps if the people in your extended family have ways to talk about what is going on, to share experiences and feelings — if everyone is too ashamed to admit to having been misused by someone with an untrustworthy hidden agenda, then no one will have the information they need to protect themselves. There is no shame in having believed someone's lies, and most of us at some time or other have given our trust to someone who turned out not to be worthy of it. It is possible to fool an honest person, but we hope you have enough humility to learn from your mistakes and not get fooled twice.

All of the above problematic scripts are about somebody not being honest, and are also about somebody having sex while avoiding intimacy and emotional connection. We prefer to trust to Nature and allow each relationship to seek its own level. That way we can discover our full potential for intimacy with each particular person, and permit each relationship to form at whatever closeness or distance is appropriate to it at any given time.

Catherine says:

Cheryl was my first female lover, and I hers. We connected almost a decade ago, and had a few months of terrific, hot sex. Unfortunately, we foundered on some difficult rocks: I was still sorting out my feelings about sex with women, and, to make matters worse, her feelings toward me became stronger and more romantic than mine toward her. We broke up in a torrent of recriminations and unhappiness. It took some time and effort, and a great deal of difficult communication, but today we're back to being the best of non-sexual friends — although we now live a couple of hours apart, we meet for a meal or an adventure every couple of months, and vacation together annually.

By treating lovers as people, and letting relationships take the shapes they want instead of the forms forced on them by the culture around them, ethical sluts can form friendships that last as sex waxes and wanes.

CHAPTER 8. ENJOYING SEX

Sex is nice and pleasure is good for you. We've said this before, and it bears repeating. In our present lives, your authors enjoy sex for its own sake, and it feels natural and comfortable, but we want you to know that it wasn't always this easy for us. In a culture that teaches that sex is sleazy, nasty, dirty and dangerous, a path to a free sexuality can be hard to find, and fraught with perils while you walk it. If you choose to walk this path, we congratulate you, and offer you support, encouragement and, most important of all, information. Start with the knowledge that we, and just about everybody else who enjoys sex without strictures, learned how to be this way despite the society we grew up in — and that means you can learn too.

WHAT IS SEX ANYWAY?

To acquire a basic knowledge of sexual functioning, and how the sexual response cycle works in men and women, we recommend strongly that you read one or several of the books in the Bibliography. Books about sex provide a lot of information — more than we can give you in a chapter — about how sex works, and what you can do about it when it isn't working as well as you'd like. Self-help exercises are usually provided for concerns about erections or orgasms, timing, coming too soon or too slow, and what to do when you can't find your turn-on. You can learn more strategies for safer sex and birth control, and more language so you can more easily talk with your partners about all of this good stuff.

We like to use an expanded definition of sex, including more than genitals, more than intercourse, more than the stimulations that lead to orgasm (and we definitely wouldn't exclude them either!). We like to think that all sensual stimulation is sexual, from a shared emotion to a shared orgasm. One friend of ours, a professional sex worker, remembers:

> I'd had a regular session with this guy once before, but one day he showed up, put $400 on the table, and said that he just wanted to talk. So we lay down together on the futon and talked all evening. It was one of the most intensely sexual experiences of my life; it felt like being in love. We were in this profound heart chakra communication, a space of pure communion that felt luscious and sweet, as thick as honey. We were close enough that we could feel the heat of each other's bodies, almost but not quite touching — we tried touching a couple of times and it diminished the energy. We were so turned on I felt nauseous. It was mind-boggling.

When we expand our concept of what sex is, and let that be whatever pleases us today, we free ourselves from the tyranny of his hydraulics, the chore of getting her off, perhaps even birth control and barriers if we decide that outercourse is perfectly good sex in and of itself.

Pleasure is good for you. So do what pleases you, and don't let anybody else tell you what you ought to like, and you can't go wrong.

Stay with what feels good and sex becomes easy, easy for yourself and incredibly easy to share with another.

Obstacles

What gets in the way of enjoying sex? Sex-negative cultural messages top the list. Many of us start out paralyzed by shame and embarrassment, even after we figure out that we don't want to be embarrassed by sex. Shame, and beliefs we were taught that our bodies, desires and sex are dirty and wrong, make it very hard to develop a healthy self-esteem. Many of us spent our adolescences consumed with guilt for our sexual desires, our fantasies and our masturbation, long before we managed to pull anything off with another human. And when we did connect with others, many of us spent those encounters obsessing about our "performance," often so convinced we were doing it wrong that we forgot to notice how good it felt.

When our desires and fantasies stretch further than a monogamous marriage with a member of the opposite sex, we suffer further attacks on our self-acceptance — we become sex-crazed perverts, the objects of scorn from others and, all too often, ourselves. According to some, even God hates us. It's hard to feel good about an expansive sexuality when you feel so bad about yourself that you just want to hide.

BODY IMAGE

None of us look sexy enough. The advertising and fashion industries see fit to line their coffers by making us all feel bad about our bodies so that we will buy more clothes, make-up, cosmetic surgery or whatever in a desperate attempt to feel okay about how we look to others. The perfume industry floods us with images designed to convince us that we smell bad (and if we smell worse than these highly merchandised scents, we must smell very bad indeed). Even those lucky souls who are young and thin and cute suffer from constant worry about how they look: why else do you think they throng to nautilus gyms and aerobic classes?

The more people you want to share sex with, the more people you are going to have to expose your naked body to, so there you are. To enjoy a free sexuality, you need to come to terms with the body you are living in, unless you want to wait till you lose twenty pounds, which could take forever, or until you look younger — don't hold your breath. Do remember: your sexiness is about how you *feel*, not how you look.

How much do you know about sex, and is it true?

Another obstacle on our course is inaccurate or just plain bad information we may have learned about sex. For many years, information about sexual behavior and basic functioning was censored, along with most other discussions of sexual pleasure. Depending on where you live in the culture now, you may or may not have access to good information. We need to politicize to protect our right to accurate and positive information about sex. Twenty-five years ago, you might not have been able to read this book. Only recently, attempts were made at the national level to censor communication on the Internet, luckily ruled unconstitutional by the courts.

Currently, books about sex proliferate, and there is much discussion on the information superhighway, and beware! — much of the information you read and hear about sex will be inaccurate. Because sexology is such a new science, and because research into what people actually do in sex is difficult and often inconclusive, *and* because we as a culture have not talked explicitly about sex for a very long time, fairy tales abound, and reality can be hard to come by. Collect all the information you can, use what works for you, and take it all with a grain of salt. Please. We have listed some of the books that we find most helpful and accurate in the Bibliography.

SPEECHLESSNESS

If you can't talk about sex, how can you think about it? The historical censorship of discussion about sex has left us with another disability: the act of talking about sex, of putting words to what we do in bed, has become difficult and embarrassing. This cuts us off from sharing about our sexual experience with our friends, sometimes even with our lovers. Think of who you would talk to if you found yourself having difficulty getting to orgasm with your partners. Would it be easy to walk up to your close friends and ask them if they ever had trouble with this? How about your partners? Although most of us have had the experience of failed sexual functioning in one way or another, most of us never get the chance to get support from our friends and lovers about it — sexual dysfunction becomes our secret shame, a position from which it is virtually impossible to figure out a way to function better.

What you can't talk about, you can hardly think about. Most of us think in words; without a language with which to speak about sex, we not only cannot communicate with others, we cannot communicate with ourselves. This is a crippling disability. What little language we have to talk about sex with is riddled with negative judgments. Either you speak in medical language of vulvas and penile intromission — which sounds like you need to be a doctor to talk about sex, so it must be a disease — or you have gutter language, fucking cunt, hard dick, that makes everything sound like an insult. When is it okay to say, "I would really love it if you ran your finger around my clit in a circle instead of up and down," or "I need you to grab my dick much harder"? As writers, we are keenly aware of how hard it is to find language to express our ideas and experiences about sex, and we have had a lot of practice.

GOAL ORIENTATION

One consequence of all the difficulties people may encounter when they set out to enjoy sex is that, driven by nervousness, they may end up acting as if their objective was to get to orgasm as rapidly as possible, as if they were trying to get it over with. When sex becomes goal-oriented, we may focus on what gets us to orgasm to the exclusion of enjoying all of the nifty sensations that come before (and, for that matter, after). When we concentrate our attention on genital sex to the exclusion of the rest of our bodies, we are excluding most of ourselves from the transaction. And when we ignore most of the good parts, we not only miss out on the good feelings, but we increase our chance of developing sexual dysfunction. And we have a lot less fun.

Skills

So how *does* a person learn about sex? The mythology has it that once we begin, it should all come naturally, and if it doesn't, then we have some deep-seated problem that only Dr. Freud can resolve. Forget this — we want to enjoy sex now, and we can't afford seven years of analysis. We advocate a simpler approach: after much research, we have come to the startling discovery that good information and willingness to learn are all you need to become the hottest lovers and have the wildest and most wonderful sex, and lots of it.

One friend of ours had her first orgasm at the age of thirty-four, after reading for the first time in one of the sex manuals which became popular in the early '70s that it was okay for her to masturbate — she'd grown up in the generation that was told that masturbation would make you sick or crazy. This makes us sick to contemplate — how many years of orgasms did this woman miss because of bad information? Nobody is born knowing how to have wonderful sex, and the information our bodies give us when we're young often gets quashed by our sex-negative culture. The best thing about learning about sex is that you'll *love* the homework — so let's get studying!

READ AND TALK

Whatever you do now you learned somewhere, somehow, so you can learn new or different sexual delights if you choose, and you can also overcome any sexual difficulties you may have. Learning requires some effort, but the rewards are great, and we know you will be brave and persistent. We recommend that you read some books about sexual functioning — our Bibliography lists good books for every lifestyle and orientation. Get your partners to read them with you, so you can all start out on the same page. Many of these books include exercises you can use to expand your sexual skills and your repertoire — try them.

Talk dirty. Talk to people about sex. Ask them about their experience, and share yours. Catherine remembers seeing her first porno movies, and feeling confounded because the women in them all masturbated face-up, and she wasn't sure if she'd been "doing it wrong" all those years. She started asking her women friends, and found that she was far from alone — not only in her face-down preference, but in her sense of uncertainty. Talk to your intimates, and any friends or people you respect who are accessible to you. Breaking the ice can be scary at first, but establishing discussion about sex with your friends and lovers will be a valuable resource for all of you, well worth risking a few minutes of embarrassment as you get started. A friend of ours used to believe that she was the only person in the whole world whose cheeks got sore from sucking cock. Talking to a few friends let her know that she was in the majority. If you find you can't talk intimately and explicitly about sex with your lovers, then how can you deal with a problem or try something new?

GOOD SEX STARTS WITH YOURSELF

We mean this quite literally. When Masters and Johnson began their research into sexual functioning in the late '50s, they wanted to start by learning about good sex before researching sexual dysfunction — so they started by selecting 382 men and 312 women, including 276 heterosexual couples, all of whom had satisfactory sex lives. One surprising fact they uncovered was that virtually all these sexually satisfied people masturbated — regardless of whether or not they were also having partnered sex.[8]

Write this on your mirror: sexually successful people masturbate. You are not making love with yourself because you are a loser, because you can't find anyone to play with you, because you are desperate to get your rocks off. You make love to yourself because you deserve pleasure, and playing with yourself makes you feel good.

People who play with themselves are good lovers for two reasons. First is that sex with yourself is a really good time to explore new sources of stimulation, like touching yourself in different places, or vibrators, or new positions, because you will never fail to notice what doesn't feel good, you will always do it the way that feels best, and there's no one to get embarrassed in front of. So masturbation offers you an opportunity to practice all sorts of interesting things: for instance, if one of your goals is too be able to enjoy more sex before you come, you can practice relaxation exercises with yourself, and learn to slow down and speed up your response however you like. And if your concern is that sometimes you are not able to come when you would like to, you can pay attention to what works for you in self-sexuality and teach your partner your individual preferences in sexual stimulation.[9] Practice makes perfect, so masturbate a lot.

Start by putting some energy into supporting your own self-esteem and developing a positive feeling about your body — no, not the body you plan to have next year after you work out every day and live on lettuce. What have you done recently that helps you feel good about the body you are inhabiting today? It's hard to have a good relationship with your body when all you do is yell at it. Try giving your body treats: a bubble bath, a trip to the hot tubs, a massage, silk underwear, anything that feels good. Be nice to your body, and then go find somebody else's body to be nice to, and somebody will be nice to your body too.

Love yourself as you would your lover. Masturbation is a good way to nourish and develop our relationships with ourselves. We can improve our self-esteem by the simple act of pleasuring our bodies. If you want a better relationship with your body, try making a date with yourself. Put your best sheets on the bed, candles and music in the bath, warm your towels, set out your sexiest nightie or robe, treat yourself to a long soak, sensuous lotion, self-massage and a dynamite climax.

We have never met a person who suffers from low self-esteem at the moment of orgasm.

Your relationship with yourself is what you bring to a relationship with another person: it is what you have to share, your offering, personally, emotionally and sexually. The sexier you are to yourself, the sexier you will be to your lovers.

And if you really want to be the world's greatest lover, and you want your partner to know exactly what pleases you the most, try masturbating in the same room. Who knows, you too might like to watch — we find it a tremendous turn-on. And in watching, or showing, you will teach and learn each other's individual pattern of pleasure, and become the most perfect, and the most perfectly satisfied lovers that ever could be.

GET YOUR CONDITIONS MET

It's hard to focus on pleasure when you're worrying about whether the baby is awake, the door is locked and the shades are drawn, or whatever bothers you. Figure out what your conditions are, what you need to feel safe and free of worry so you can enjoy your sex completely. Deal with your needs beforehand. Establish your agreements with your partner about safer sex and/or birth control. It is not appropriate to argue with anyone's limits regarding pregnancy and disease risk reduction: respect the limits of the most conservative person, because sex is a lot more fun when we all feel safe. Personal limits may be idiosyncratic, and that's okay too. Dossie has a minor obsession about being clean, and likes to set up clean sheets and have a shower so she feels all fresh and sparkly. Someone else might not care as much — so what? There is no one right way to get ready to have sex. Give yourself permission to take care of your own needs; it will free you.

Sometimes you discover that your conditions aren't what you thought they were, and that the new ones might offer some special fun. Catherine remembers:

> I'd been to a concert that night with two friends, who were lovers of each other's and of mine. One of us had recently acquired a treasure: a '64 Lincoln Continental the size of a studio apartment. On the way back, we decided to stop by the river to admire the moonlight, and before we knew it we were throwing a full-scale orgy in the front seat of the Lincoln. I'd always thought I wouldn't like sex in a car, but when I found myself stretched out in the front seat with my head in one partner's lap as I masturbated him over my shoulder, and my other partner kneeling in the passenger footwell with her head buried between my legs, I began to change my mind. The scene ended in hysterical giggles: the one I was masturbating began to come, his body went into an orgasmic spasm, and he hit the horn — the car emitted an enormous blast of sound from its mid-'60s Detroit horn that must have awakened everybody for miles around, and made us all practically fall out of our seat!

COMMUNICATE

Most of us have been struck dumb by the scariest communication task of all — asking for what we want. Is there any one of us who has never failed to tell our partner when we want our clit or cock stimulated harder or softer, slower or faster, more on the shaft or more on the tip, on the side, on both sides, up and down or round about, or whatever it is that would work for us? Take it from us, the way to get what you want in sex is to ask for it. And the way to get a good reputation as an excellent lover is to ask each partner what he or she likes, and let them show you how to do it exactly right: Catherine makes a point of having her lovers masturbate for her early on in the relationship, so she can watch how they do it and make mental notes about what kinds of stimulation they like to feel. Once you get past the initial embarrassment, this is actually easy, and will make you a very popular lover indeed.

If you find this impossibly difficult, we have an idea that will help. Try this exercise with yourself or with a lover that you are very familiar with, and as you get comfortable, repeat it with each new lover.

First, make a list of all the sexual activities you can think of that anyone, not just you, might like to do. You will immediately discover that this is also an exercise in developing language, so pay attention as you name these things. Are you more comfortable with intercourse or fucking, oral sex, going down, cocksucking or eating out? What do you call your own sex organs — penis, dick, cock, prick... pussy, cunt, vagina, clitoris? If you get stuck, put a little effort into finding any name that describes the activity, take a deep breath and repeat those words five times, and breathe again. Make your list as complete as possible, and include activities that you don't like as well as those you do. You can make this list by yourself, with a partner or a friend, or with a group of people who may or may not be your lovers. When you make the list of all possible sex acts with a group of people, you get good practice in talking about sex explicitly, graphically and on purpose.

Then each person takes a separate sheet of paper and makes three columns: YES, NO and MAYBE. YES means I like this, NO means I don't want to do this, and MAYBE means maybe if I felt safe enough, or was turned on enough, or my partner were very experienced, or whatever. Make your personal list privately, and share with your partner or partners after. When you are negotiating an evening's entertainment, everything on the NO lists is off limits, everything on both partner's YES list is the wonderful fun you are ready to share. And if all goes well, you may get to try out an item or two from the MAYBE list. We strongly encourage you to try this exercise — you will be amazed at how much you will learn, and how easy communication can be once you get started.

We have also included on Page 102 an inventory of sexual activities. Try filling it out and see what you learn about yourself. You can make copies to share with your friends as an ice-breaker for a discussion group or for negotiating a sexual encounter. We made the boxes as big as possible so you can make comments about how you feel, which tends to be more informative than a simple yes or no.

These are ideas about how you can start communicating explicitly about sex, and negotiate consensuality. Remember, we define consent as an active collaboration for the pleasure, benefit and well-being of all persons concerned. This means that everybody involved must agree to whatever activity is proposed, and must also feel safe enough that they could decline if they wished. We believe that if you are not free to say "no," you can't really say "yes." We also think it is essential that everyone involved understands the consequences of both responses, which is another way of saying that it's not acceptable to take advantage of someone's naïveté.

YOUR S[

	sex with opposite sex	sex with same sex	sex with a younger person	sex with an older person	group sex	masturbation alone	masturbation with par[	nude n[
never even thought about								
ever fantasized or imagined								
fantasize now								
would like to try								
have tried								
will never try								
liked								
disliked								
part of my sexual pattern								
would like to add to my sexual pattern								

Some possible responses: yuck!   hmmm...   !!!

VENTORY

	oral sex - active	oral sex - receptive	vaginal penetration - active	vaginal penetration - receptive	anal penetration - active	anal penetration - receptive	vibrators & toys	S/M - active	S/M - receptive

Ouch!　　???　　Eeek!　　HOT!!!　　Scary　　Hmmm...

We cannot say this often enough: You have a right to your limits and it is totally okay to say no to any form of sex you don't like or are not comfortable with. Having a limit does not mean that you are inhibited, uptight, no fun, or a permanent victim of American puritanism. It just means you don't like something, and if you want to learn to like it, we think there are better ways to do that than to succumb to guilt-tripping, shaming or outright bullying. Say no to what you don't want, and when you decide to try something new, arrange for lots of support from your partner, get your conditions met, and be kind to yourself. Positive reinforcement is really the best way to learn.

In many areas, workshops and groups about sex are available, put on by dedicated sex educators and counselors, sometimes at birth control clinics or organizations supporting sexual health. All of these workshops are designed to be safe, to respect everyone's boundaries and give you an opportunity to learn new information, increase your comfort level and speak for yourself about your own feelings and experience. What we are advocating here is communication by, with and for everybody.

FIND YOUR TURN-ON

Have you ever set out to make love and discovered that you couldn't find your turn-on? There you are, hunting for that elusive state of excitement, and wondering what's wrong with you when your lover does the things you usually love and your response is just plain nothing, or worse yet, irritation or ticklishness. Women wonder why they aren't getting wet, men agonize over absent erections, everybody either fakes it or gets embarrassed. It happens to everybody. Really. It's not just you.

For some people, losing their turn-on happens when they are nervous, maybe with a new partner or in a new situation. For others, familiarity reduces arousal, and they have a hard time grasping their desire in the relationships with the people they know the best and love the most.

Lust for one person is seldom satisifed by sex with another, but experienced sluts know that turn-on is transferable. The excitement you feel about the sex you're planning with Bill next weekend can easily set a fire under your session with Jane tonight, because arousal is a physical experience that can be used for anything you want. The lust in the mind persists, and will still be there for you when you get around to Bill — we promise.

Getting turned on requires a physical and mental transition into a different state of consciousness. Every night, when you go to sleep, you make such a transition: you turn the lights down, get into loose clothing, lie down, perhaps read quietly or watch a little TV, deliberately changing your state of consciousness from wide awake to sleepy. Some people do this automatically, while others have to work at figuring out what helps them get to sleep.

Similarly, we all need to know how we get turned on, what works for us when arousal doesn't just come of its own accord. Our mythology tells us that we are not supposed to have to do this on purpose, that we are supposed to be swept away with desire, or else something is wrong: we don't really want to make love to this person, we've made a terrible mistake and now what are we going to do with the kids? Men are told that they are supposed to be so turned on by the mere availability of a partner that their erection should stand up and salute without any actual sensory stimulation. Women are taught that they ought to be turned on in response to any stimulus from a partner they care about, and if they aren't, they are frigid or perhaps feeling hostile. These are only some of the very destructive lessons you may have learned.

So the first thing you need to do when desire doesn't come up like thunder is to remember that lots of serious sluts have dealt with this problem successfully, and so can you. So let's look at how we could go about getting turned on on purpose.

Some people just charge on, start sexual stimulation and keep on with it until their turn-on catches up with them, and this works for many people much of the time. Dossie once had a partner who liked to leap into cold mountain lakes when they were camping, insisting that you'd get warm eventually if you just thrash around.

Other people like to get in one step at a time, warming up gradually and sensually, allowing time to appreciate the changes in sensitivity that occur as they move slowly into their sexual response cycle. For many people, simply slowing down gives them the chance to get in synch with their turn-on, and once you find your turnon it makes it easier to speed up.

Many people experience hypersensitivity, which means feeling ticklish or jumpy or irritated, when they attempt to take in sensations that are too focused or too intense in the early part of their journey to arousal. Such ticklishness usually disappears once the person is thoroughly excited, and may reappear right after orgasm. The only way to deal with hypersensitivity is to remember that almost nobody can get turned on while they are being tickled or irritated, so take your time. (Dossie's partner who loved to leap into cold lakes also really loved to be tickled, but Dossie hates it, so Dossie didn't get tickled and her girlfriend did. Diversity rules.) Feel free to tell your lover about hypersensitivity, and what sensations you enjoy early on, and how that may be different later. Most hypersensitivity can be cured with a firm touch and a gradual approach. Start with caressing backs and shoulders and less sensitive parts of the body, making sure of serious arousal before touching the more exquisitely sensitive areas.

Talk with your lover about what turns you on — a fantasy? A story? Having your fingers or toes gently bitten and sucked? Ask your lover what turns him on — chewing on a neck? Brushing his hair? You could prepare for this talk by writing down a list of all the things that you know excite you, each of you on your own, and then sharing your lists. Talking can be a little risky, and risk can be exciting in and off itself.

Get into your body: sensual delights like hot tubs, bubble baths, naked skin by the warm fire, massage. These are the slower delights that give us time to focus our attention on physical pleasure, and allow our busy brains to slow down or drift off into fantasy. This kind of pleasure should not be demanding, this is not the time to worry about heavy breathing or undulating hips. This is the time for entrancement.

Fantasy is a big turn-on for many people, and yes, it is perfectly normal to fantasize when your partner is doing sexy things to you. Many people also like to fantasize on their own before their erotic encounters, building up a nice head of steam before any touching actually takes place. Perhaps you would both enjoy watching an erotic video, or reading each other grown-up bedtime stories. Maybe it would be hot to tell each other your favorite fantasies.

Excitement begins with a slow sensual warmth, and when the warm-up has begun, the door is open for more intense excitement, exploring the sensitivities of ears, necks, wrists and toes, or tongues in mouths. Breathing becomes deeper, and hips start to move of their own accord.

So does this excitement mean it's time to leap on that express train to orgasmic release? Just because your body is physically ready to enjoy sex doesn't mean you need to rush to fulfillment! Why don't you take a little more time? This feels good, right? So what about feeling good a little more, getting a little more turned on: remember when you were in high school and you could neck for hours?

SLOW DOWN

And don't we all want a lover with a slow hand? The most common mistake people make when they get nervous about sex is to rush things. Tension does tend to speed us up, and it is also true that both men and women develop a lot of muscle tension as they approach orgasm, which adds to the furor. Now when we are truly ready, there is nothing we like more than to grunt and gasp and heave and shout and make fists with our toes on the speeding express train to orgasm. But there is more to sex than orgasm, so let's not leave out sensuality, seduction, the oh-so-gradual turn-on, the building of suspense, the exploration of every part of the body that can arouse the senses — we want to do it all. And to explore the entire range of sensual and sexual intimacy, we need to learn techniques for slowing down.

The first technique for slowing down is very simple. Take a deep breath and hold it. Put your hand on your abdomen and feel the hardness of your muscles. Then breathe out, slowly, and you will feel the muscles in your torso relax. When we are tense, we tend to breathe in gasps, gulping air in and exhaling very little, and that's how we maintain tension in our muscles and in our minds. When we breathe out, we relax. So anytime you are tense, in any situation, you can relax a little by taking three long, slow, deep breaths, making sure to breathe out as thoroughly as you breathe in.

You can reduce your nervousness about talking about sex, and you can slow yourself down during sex, just by breathing. When you slow your breathing while you are turned on, let your awareness go down into your body. Scan your whole body with your mind, starting from your toes, and let yourself notice how each part of you feels. Chances are you will discover a lot of good feelings you hadn't even felt before. Sex therapists call this sensate focus, and advocate it in particular for those who want to slow down their response and enjoy more sex before they come. You can slow down your physical sexual response by breathing, relaxing and focusing your attention to reduce your physical tension, because, you see, not only do we all tense our muscles before we come, but most of us cannot come when our muscles are relaxed. So orgasmic control is not achieved by grunting and bearing down, but rather by relaxing and enjoying yourself.

Slowing down is also useful when you are trying out new activities, or nervous for any reason. Our friend Mandy relates one of her early learning experiences with condoms:

> Rob and I had been occasional lovers for many years, and we were getting together for the first time after a long hiatus. We had very little experience of safer sex at the time, but decided, due to our various experiences, that if we wanted to fuck we should use a condom. This was all fine in theory, but when the time came to put it on after a suitable and exciting round or two of

outercourse, Rob picked up that difficult little piece of rubber and promptly lost his erection. I'm sure this has never happened to any of you.

We fooled around for a little while, and tried again, with the same response — Rob's mind and his cock were not in agreement, and his cock was not cooperating. I dragged myself up into a more active consciousness and decided to put what I had learned in adult sex education to use.

I got him to lie back and agree to be done to, and I set up the environment: candles for light carefully placed where we wouldn't knock them over, lubricant and towels handy, and two or three rubbers in case we broke one, plus slow sensual music on a long tape. I got myself in a comfortable position between his legs — comfortable because I wanted to take all the time in the world, and I did not want to be interrupted by an aching back or a cramped shoulder.

I started by stroking his body — thighs, tummy, legs — very gently, in a soothing way, for a long time, till he first relaxed, and then responded with an erection. I waited a little longer so he could enjoy that erection without any responsibility for taking things further: in sex therapy, this is called non-demand pleasuring. Then I moved the stroking to his genitals around, but not on his penis. His erection went down again, so I moved further back and continued sensual stroking on his skin until he got hard again, and continued again a little longer, and then moved to touching closer to his cock. This time his erection fell only a little, and got hard again after only a few seconds. By now he was breathing hard, and so was I. For me, the experience was very sensual and kind of trancelike, warm and pleasurable: a major turn-on too.

I spent a very long time stroking around, but not on, his cock, until he was very hard indeed. He reached for me, but I slapped his hand — no distractions, please. I am doing this to you, get it? When the suspense was virtually unbearable, I ran my hand lightly over his dick — he shuddered. Stroking his cock and pulling gently on his balls aroused him even more, and he was beginning to moan and sweat. I picked up the condom, checking to make sure I was unrolling it in the right direction, and he lost his erection almost instantly. I went back to stroking around, not on, his cock, and he sprang up again, getting impatient but I made him wait, played with his dick for a long time but gently enough that I knew he couldn't come.

The next time I approached with the rubber, he only wilted a tiny bit, so I rubbed a bit more, and we went round a few times until he was so turned on he couldn't think any more and his cock stood up nice and straight while I rolled the rubber over it. I continued playing with him while he got used to the new sensation.

By this time I was seriously turned on and more than a little impatient, so when I gave the word, he attacked

and did the raging bull thing, and we both finally got to
fuck fast and hard: well worth the waiting, I say. You
should have seen the explosion, I'm sure they heard us
in the next town.

To sum up, and maybe catch our breath a little ourselves, a basic skill for good sex is knowing how to relax, and slow down, and then knowing how to tense and speed up. And once you know how, you can go round and round as many times as you can bear to hold off, enjoying every minute and building up excitement for the grand finale. Relaxing your breathing, and relaxing your body, can help you get centered, grounded in your body and in the pleasure you are feeling, and give you more choices about your sex. You can learn more about relaxation and slowing down by taking a class in any form of yoga, practicing sensual massage, trying tantric techniques, or just slowing down long enough to discover what fun it is to focus on what you're feeling when you're feeling good.

PART II – BETWEEN ONE ANOTHER

CHAPTER 1. BOUNDARIES

Many people believe that to be a slut is to be indiscriminate, to not care about who you make love with, and thus to not care about yourself. They believe that we live in excessively wide open spaces, with no discrimination, no fences, no boundaries. Nothing could be further from the truth. To be an ethical slut you need to have very good boundaries that are clear, strong, flexible, and, above all, conscious.

One very successful slut we interviewed is outraged by accusations of indiscrimacy, and points out that sluts get a great deal of opportunity to develop exquisitely sophisticated discrimination: "We actually have *more* boundaries than most folks because we have more points of contact," more experience relating in very different ways to very diverse people.

What Are Boundaries?

It is basic to any relationship, and particularly important in open relationships, that no one can own another person. Ownership is not what relationships are about. We each own ourselves, lock, stock and barrel. We each have the responsibility of living our own lives, determining our individual needs and arranging to get those needs met. We cannot live through a partner, nor can we assume that just because we have a lover, all of our needs should automatically be satisfied. Many of us have been taught that if our lover does not meet every need, this must not be true love, our lover must be somehow inadequate, or we must be at fault — too needy or undeserving or some other judgment like that.

If you were brought up to believe that your relationship would provide your other, or (shudder) better half, or that your destiny is to submerge your identity in a relationship, you will probably have to put some attention into learning about your own boundaries. Boundaries are invariably in the plural because none of them hold still for long and all of them are individual. They are how we understand where you begin and I end, where and how we are separate as individuals. You need to figure out where your limits are, what constitutes comfortable distance or closeness between yourself and others in various situations, and particularly the ways in which you and your lovers are different and individual and unique.

If you read the literature about codependency, or attend support groups with Codependents Anonymous, you can learn more about how to own your own life, how to get into that position of ownership, and the ways in which we all often fail to do so — mostly by understanding the complexities of boundaries.

Owning Your Choices

It is axiomatic in communication between intimates that each person owns their own emotions, and that each person is responsible for dealing with those emotions. This means that nobody "makes" you feel anything. If someone yells at you, for instance, you have emotional choices: you might feel afraid, or angry, or icy calm. You also have behavioral choices: you might decide to yell back, or leave, or get closer and resolve this problem right now because you can't stand it. And all of these, and the many other responses too numerous to mention here, belong to you.

Nobody makes anybody feel anything. Understanding this is the first step to claiming something very precious — your own emotions. And when you grasp your emotions, you have something unbelievably valuable to bring to your relationships.

When you find yourself responding to someone else's behavior, it is easy to dwell on what they have done and how terrible it is and what exactly *they* should do to fix it. Instead, try looking at your own feelings as a true message about your internal state of being, and decide how *you* want to deal with whatever's going on. Do you want to find out more? Do you want to discuss a limit? Do you want a little time to yourself to calm down and get centered? Do you want to be heard about something? When you take responsibility, you get these choices, and more.

What you are *not* responsible for is your lover's emotions. You can choose to be supportive — we're great believers in the healing power of listening — but it is not your job to fix anything.

Once you understand that your lover's emotions are not your job or your fault, you can listen to him and really hear what he has to say, without falling victim to an overwhelming need to figure out whose fault it is or to make the emotion change or go away.

Some people tend to respond to a lover's pain and confusion with an intense desire to fix something. "Fix-it" messages can feel like invalidation to the person who is trying to express an emotion. "Why don't you just do this... try that... forget about it... relax!" sends the message that the person expressing the emotion has overlooked some obvious and simple solution and is an idiot for feeling bad in the first place. Such messages disempower and invalidate him.

It is up to each of us to fix how we feel, to reach out for the support and connection we want, and to set our own limits about what we don't want in our lives right now. In this way, we all get to solve problems in our relationships, learn about ourselves and get along much better with all of our partners.

RELATIONSHIP BOUNDARIES

Relationships also have boundaries. The agreements that free-loving couples and families make with respect for each other's feelings constitute the boundaries of their relationship. In an open sexual community, it is important to deal with each relationship within its own boundaries. That means, for example, that you figure out your limits with your partner before you go to the sex party, that you don't use your mistress to diss your wife, that decisions are made with input from everybody affected by them — which means not behind anybody's back — and so on.

Communities based on sex and intimacy work best when everybody has respect for everybody's relationships, which includes not only lovers, but children and families of origin and neighbors and exes and so on. Such communities can evolve into highly connected family systems when everyone is conscious of and caring about boundaries.

Problems With Boundaries

Learn from your mistakes. Boundaries can get tricky at times, so we hope you give yourselves lots of slack to explore and have your trials and make your errors, and learn from them. Remember, you can't learn from your errors if you always gotta be right!

DUMPING

One place where people often get confused is differentiating between the honest sharing of feelings and dumping. Dumping means using another person as your garbage pit, spewing your problematic stuff all over her and leaving it there. Asking someone to listen to your feelings is different from dropping them in his lap and leaving them there. Dumping usually carries the expectation that the dumpee will *do* something about the problem, even if it's simply to take on the burden of worrying so that the dumper can stop. Usually you can avoid dumping by making it totally clear that your need to share your emotional state carries no obligation for your listener: "I don't like your having a date with Paula tonight," followed by a heavy and pregnant silence, carries an entirely different weight than "I'm feeling a little insecure about your date with Paula tonight, but I want you to go ahead and have it. Are you okay with listening to some of my fears? Can we talk a bit about ways that I might be able to feel safer?"

PROJECTION

Another trick to watch out for — no, not the kind you find at the disco on Saturday night! — is projection. Projection is when we use another person as a screen to run our movie on. We see our fantasy, and miss the real person. We imagine we know his thoughts, when in fact we are thinking about our fears. We predict that she will respond the same way our parents did — "I know you'll reject me if I don't make a lot of money," "You'll never respect me if I show you my sadness." Or we might be projecting our expectations, projections that our lovers — who are not mind-readers — can never live up to: "You're supposed to take care of me!" "Whaddaya mean, you're not horny? *I'm* horny!"

When you make a commitment to own your own stuff, you can stop projecting and see the people you love clearly in all their glory. When all of you work together to own your stuff, each of you, then you will never again feel like a puppet in somebody else's show.

Role boundaries

This boundary may seem unfamiliar because we don't have that much experience with living in multiple relationships. You may find yourself playing out different roles, indeed feeling like a somewhat different person, with different partners. With one partner you might feel young and vulnerable and protected; with another, you are Earth mother. With one lover you might feel careful and solid and safe, with another you might be dashing and reckless.

Catherine got a wonderful feeling of acceptance for all her parts from a recent moment:

> I enjoy games in which I role-play the part of a "little
> girl," but my regular partner isn't comfortable with them.
> After a bit of searching, though, I found within my circle
> of acquaintances a man who enjoys being a "Daddy" as
> much as I enjoy having one. My partner was delighted
> I'd found a safe place to play that role, and we both felt
> I'd made a good choice in selecting someone to whom I
> could entrust such vulnerable parts of me. "Daddy" and I
> get together once or twice a month for finger-painting,
> watching Disney movies, eating peanut butter sand-
> wiches, and other slightly more adult pleasures.
>
> Recently I attended a party where both my life partner
> and my "daddy" were in attendance. From across the

room, I saw the two of them chatting, and I headed over to say hi. As I drew closer, my partner held his arm out invitingly and called, "Hey, hon, come over here and hang out with your dad and your boyfriend for a while."
The feeling of acceptance, and the warmth of knowing the two men accepted and honored each other's role in my life, was amazing.

One of the things people get out of multiple relationships is the chance to be all of their various selves. When two people meet, they relate where they intersect, where they have complementary roles in similar scripts. So, being different things to different lovers, we might find ourselves having different boundaries, limits and relationship styles in different circumstances.

This might manifest in a variety of ways. For instance, I might be calm and centered when Lover A is angry, but Lover B's irritability is distressing to me — it "pushes my buttons," perhaps reminding me of a past lover or a punitive parent. In this case, I need to own my buttons, and figure out if my limits with Lover B are going to be different from my limits with Lover A.

Forget about fairness. Ethical sluttery does not mean that all things come out equal. Different relationships have different boundaries, different limits, and different potentials. So if your lover has found someone that she can share a certain activity with, and you would like to share that with her too, the question is not "Why don't you do that with me?" but "That sounds interesting, how do you suppose we could make that work for us?"

This is how one woman we interviewed put it:

My open sexual lifestyle gives me personal freedom, independence, and responsibility in a way that being an exclusive couple doesn't. Because I'm responsible, every day, for my needs being met (or not), and for creating and maintaining the relationships in my life, I can take nothing for granted. Every person I meet has the potential for whatever it is that's right between me and that person, regardless of how my relationships are with anybody else. And so this lifestyle gives me a very concrete feeling of individuality, that I recreate every day. I feel more like a grownup, adult, responsible person when I know that my life, all of it, who I fuck, who I relate to, how I relate to them, is all my choice. I promised my partner that I would share my life with him, and that implies to me that I have a life to share — a complete life. And it's clear to me that he's here because he wants to be, wherever "here" is. We are with each other, every day, because we really want to be. Our choices are real.

CHAPTER 2. SLUT ECONOMIES

As we have said before, many traditional attitudes about sexuality are based on the idea that there isn't enough of something — love, sex, friendship, commitment — to go around. If you believe this, if you think that there's a limited amount of what you want, it can seem very important to stake your claim to your share of it. You may believe that you have to take your share away from somebody else, since if it's all that good a thing someone else probably already has it (how unfair!). Or you may believe that if someone else gets something, that means there must be less of it for you.

STARVATION ECONOMIES

We call this kind of thinking "starvation economies." People often learn about starvation economies in childhood, when parents who are emotionally depleted or unavailable teach us that we must work hard to get our emotional needs met — so that if we relax our vigilance for even a moment, a mysterious someone or something may take the love we need away from us. Some of us may even have experienced real-world hunger (if you didn't grab first, your brother got all the potatoes), or outright neglect, deprivation or abuse. We may learn starvation economies later in life, from manipulative, withholding or punitive lovers, spouses or friends.

The beliefs acquired in childhood usually run deep, both in individuals and in our culture. So you may have to look carefully to see the pattern. You can see it in a small way in the kind of "complaining contests" some people engage in: "Boy, did I have a rotten day today." "You think *your* day was rotten — wait till you hear about *my* day!" — as though there were a limited amount of sympathy in the world, and the only way to get the amount due you was to compete for it. People may think that if you love Bill that means you must love Mary less, or if you're committed to your relationship with your friend you must be less committed to your relationship with your spouse.

This kind of thinking is a trap. We know, for example, that having a second child doesn't usually mean that a parent loves the first child less, and that the person who owns three pets doesn't necessarily give any less care to each one than the person who owns one. But when it comes to sex, particularly sex with a romantic component, it's hard for most people to believe that more for you doesn't mean less for me.

LETTING GO

Getting over past fears of starvation can be one of the biggest challenges of ethical sluthood. It requires an enormous leap of faith — you have to let go of some of what feels like yours, trusting that it will be replaced, and more, by a generous world. You need to get clear that you deserve love and nurturance and warmth and sex. And if the world hasn't been all that generous to you in the past, this may be very difficult.

Unfortunately, we can't promise you that the world *will* be generous to you. We think it will — that if you loosen your possessive grip on the love that's already yours, you'll get more, from the person who loves you, and maybe from some other people too. It certainly has worked for us. But, especially in the beginning, letting go of false starvation economies can feel a lot like trapeze-swinging — letting go of what you already have (or believe that you have), trusting that at the end of the leap there will always be something else to grab.

Is there a safety net for this kind of daredevilry? Well, yes, but it's going to require another leap of faith... because the safety net is *you*. Your self-reliance, your self-nurturing, your ability to spend time in your own company. If being alone seems unbearable to you, the courage required to relinquish what's "yours," the things that stand between you and aloneness, may be impossible to summon.

On the other hand, what an incredibly free feeling it is to realize that there *is* enough love, sex, commitment, support and nurturing to go around! Catherine used to spend the nights when her partner was out with someone else by getting together with one of her own other lovers, so she wouldn't have to be alone. Now, she says, "I know that option is there for me if I want it — but more often I choose to spend that time in my own company, enjoying the opportunity for solitary self-indulgence." Knowing that the world offers plenty of companionship, she feels safe enough to not need that reassurance.

REAL-WORLD LIMITS

In contrast to starvation economies, some of the things we want really *are* limited. There are only twenty-four hours in the day, for example — so trying to find enough time to do all the wonderfully slutty things you enjoy, with all the people you care about, can be a real challenge (and sometimes may simply not be possible).

- **Time** is the biggest real-world limit we encounter in trying to live and love as we like. This problem is hardly exclusive to sluts; monogamous folks run into problems finding the time for sex, companionship and communication, too. Careful planning can help — if you don't already keep a fairly detailed datebook or computerized calendar, now is a good time to start. Respecting one another's realities, and staying flexible, is important. Crises happen: a sick child, a work emergency, or even another partner who needs companionship and reassurance during a particularly bad time. You might also want to do some thinking about how much time you need to get your needs met: do you really have to stay over and have breakfast together the next day, or would an hour or two of cuddling and talk be just as nice?

However you work out your schedule, remember that everybody concerned needs to know about it, and that may include more people than you are used to thinking about. A friend of ours, having failed to inform his wife's lover about an engagement that affected her schedule, moaned: "I know I told *someone!*"

Don't forget to schedule time to relate to your partner and play with your kids. And don't leave yourself out: many busy sluts find it important to schedule alone time for rest and replenishment. Catherine, who lives in a Grand Central Station-like group household, has an arrangement with her girlfriend that she can occasionally use Barbara's house for solitary retreats — a rare and precious gift — while Barbara is out of town.

• **Space** is another real-world limit for many people. Few of us are fortunate enough to live in multi-room mansions with rooms dedicated exclusively to sex. If you're in your bedroom with your friend, and your live-in partner is sleepy and wants to go to bed, you've got a problem. Crashing on a narrow couch in your own apartment, while your partner disports with someone else in your bed, may be beyond the limits of even the most advanced slut. This problem may be solved by separate bedrooms or personal spaces if you can afford them. One couple we interviewed said, "Having separate bedrooms is a non-negotiable need for us; we wouldn't be able to maintain this lifestyle without them." Sometimes a hotel room or other rented or borrowed space can be another good solution. If neither of these is an option, we suggest making clear agreements about what times the shared space is available for other-partner sex, and sticking strictly to them.

• **Things.** It's only natural to want to share our possessions with the people we care about. But this urge can cause problems when possessions — money, food, art, toys — belong, legally or emotionally, to more than one person. If there's any chance that someone feels a sense of possession about an item, we strongly recommend that you talk carefully with that person before you share the item with someone else. This rule is sometimes simple: you don't let your lover polish off the carton of milk that your spouse was planning to drink for breakfast. But it sometimes gets tricky, too. While you may have the legal right to give away a gift that was given to you by someone else, the wife who sees her husband's Father's Day tie around his lover's neck may feel understandably miffed. (These are some of the advanced boundaries we told you about.) Similarly, it's not a good idea to share with someone else an item that was made for you by a lover, or that the two of you bought together during an intimate shopping trip. Many sluts, for the purposes of hygiene and/or emotional attachment, set aside certain sex toys for use with only one person: *my* vibrator, *Harry's* dildo. Lending or giving jointly owned money without discussing it with the co-owner is, we hope it's not necessary to say, unacceptable.

- **"The tyranny of hydraulics."** This is Dossie's phrase for the biological realities that govern many aspects of sexuality. While it might be nice to think that you're a sexual superman who can generate erections on demand *ad infinitum*, neither of us has yet met such a man. A partner who is looking forward to conventional sexual activities with a male lover may be quite understandably disappointed to find him unavailable by virtue of having ejaculated with another partner earlier that day. And even the most multiply orgasmic of women can't stay turned on forever.

Such problems can often be solved by readjusting your expectations of what constitutes "sex" — does it *really* always require an erection? An orgasm? An ejaculation? Practitioners of tantric yoga have developed ways by which many men can experience orgasm without ejaculation. These strategies are only somewhat useful for birth control and safer sex, and are certainly no substitute for rubbers. But they come with a wonderful side effect: men who learn to orgasm without ejaculating are able to come many times, like women. And practitioners of many other kinds of sex have developed ways in which enthusiastic sluts can give their partners one or many orgasms, regardless of their own state of arousal. Before you give up on polyamory because of "the tyranny of hydraulics," we suggest you investigate at least some of these possibilities (our earlier chapter on Enjoying Sex, and some of the books in the Bibliography, will help).

Remember outercourse. Remember sensuality. Rediscover massage for its own sake. Share a seriously filthy conversation about what you'd like to do to each other tomorrow.

AM I REALLY GOING TO STARVE?

When you try to decide what limits you want to the openness of your relationship, it's not always easy to tell which fears are based on reality and which on fear or illusion. First, you have to pinpoint the areas in your life where you feel insecure, where you perceive the possibility of deprivation — which requires a lot of self-searching and honesty. It helps to ask, "What am I afraid might happen?"

Is my partner's fondness for his friend really going to make him fall out of love with me? What if my partner doesn't think I'm special any more? What if she's so ecstatically happy that she doesn't need me? Why would she ever want me, anyway? These are some of the horrible little thoughts that pop up in all of our minds when we're scared of starving.

You need to decide whether your fear is a possible reality, or something that probably wouldn't happen. Frequent check-ins, good communication to keep you aware of whether anyone's feeling deprived or overextended, and lots of internal reality checks (is your disappointment that he couldn't get it up really just that, or is it anger or jealousy over his date last night?) can help. We'll talk later about how to get reassurance when you're afraid.

LIMITS CAN STRETCH

Sometimes, you just have to try it and see. The old chestnut about "If you love something, let it go" is sentimental, but more than a kernel of truth lies at its core. In the same way that a dieter is sometimes counseled to let himself get hungry in order to see what that feels like, you may need to let yourself feel deprived, simply to prove to yourself that feeling deprived isn't the end of the world. Sometimes letting go of one pleasure opens your eyes to another that was there from the start; sometimes a new one comes along; sometimes you find out you don't need it all that much right now anyway. We can't tell you what letting go will feel like; all we can do is assure you that you will learn something from it. Scary... and satisfying!

A song to remember:

Love is a rose and you better not pick it
Only grows when it's on the vine
Handful of thorns and you know you missed it
Lose your love when you say the word "mine."[10]

CHAPTER 3. JEALOUSY

"Let jealousy be your teacher. Jealousy can lead you
to the very places where you most need healing. It can
be your guide into your own dark side and show you the
way to total self-realization. Jealousy can teach you how
to live in peace with yourself and with the whole world
if you let it." — Deborah Anapol, Love Without Limits

For many people, the biggest obstacle to free love is the emotion
we call jealousy.

Jealousy feels really rotten and most of us will go to great lengths
to avoid feeling it. However, your authors believe that most people take
the destructive power of jealousy way too much for granted, that they
give their jealousy far more power than it deserves. After many years of
living free and dealing successfully with jealousy, we tend to forget that
we live in a culture that considers it acceptable to divorce or even murder
a sexually explorative partner who has committed the unthinkable crime
of arousing jealousy in us. We danced happily for years to a bouncy
Beatles tune before we noticed the lyrics that threatened, "I'd rather
see you dead, little girl, than to see you with another man..."

Let us point out here that monogamy is not a cure for jealousy.
Joe managed to get pathologically jealous without Dossie ever cheating.
We have all had experiences of being ferociously jealous of work that

keeps our partner away or distracted from us, or of our lover's decision to cruise the Internet instead of our bodies, or of Monday (and Tuesday and Wednesday and...) Night Football. Jealousy is not exclusive to sluts; it's an emotion we all have to deal with in our relationships.

Many people believe that sexual territoriality is a natural part of individual and social evolution, and use jealousy as justification to go berserk, and stop being a sane, responsible and ethical human being. Threatened with feeling jealous, we allow our brains to turn to static on the excuse that we are acting on instinct.

What Is Jealousy?

We cannot ask this question too often. What is jealousy to you? Does jealousy really exist, and is it what we think it is? Once we are willing to confront the feeling of jealousy rather than run away from it, we can see more clearly what jealousy truly is for each of us. Jealousy may be an expression of insecurity, of fear of rejection, fear of abandonment, feeling left out, feeling not good enough, or feeling inadequate.

Sometimes what we perceive as jealousy is actually something else. Think through the details of how jealousy works with you. What bothers you the most? Is it that you don't want her to do those things to someone else, or that you *do* want her to do them to you? Jealousy might actually be envy, and envy is often very easy to fix: why not make a date with your lover to do what you have just discovered you are missing?

Sometimes jealousy has at its roots feelings of grief and loss, which can be harder to interpret. We have been taught by our culture that when our partner has sex with another, we have lost something. Not to sound dumb, but we are confused. What have we lost? When our partner comes home from a hot date with another, often she is excited, turned on and has some new ideas she would like to try out at home. We fail to see what we lose in this situation.

On the other hand, sometimes the truth is that we are becoming aware on an intuitive level that our partner is moving away from us, and it might be true that we are losing the relationship that we cherish. That does happen. And the fact that supposedly monogamous people everywhere often leave one partner for what they perceive as greener grass with another is not much consolation when it happens to you.

We watched a friend of ours go through feelings of deep grief and loss when she perceived that her partner's lover was trying, quite nearly successfully, to abscond with him. In this case, her pain threw a spotlight on some dishonesty and manipulation on the part of the third party, and gave her partner the strength to break off from the lover and to find other lovers who had greater respect for his primary bond. On the other hand, this scenario might just as easily have ended in a breakup; we'll talk more about breakups, and dealing with them ethically with care for your own and your partner's feelings, in the chapter on "Sluts In Love."

Jealousy might also be associated with feelings of competitiveness and wanting to be number one. Dossie's daughter, when young, once asked her, "If there were an Olympics of sex would you win a gold medal?" We say thank the Goddess there is no Olympics of sex, because sexual achievement is not measurable — so get that ruler out of here. We cannot rank each and every one of us on some hierarchical ladder of who is or is not the most desirable, or the better fuck. What a horrid idea! We want to live in a world where each person's sexuality is valued for its own sake, not for how it measures up to any standard beyond our own pleasure. And if you learn from someone else's experience something that you would like to add to your own repertoire of skills, you can certainly learn to do it without wasting time trashing yourself for not already having known how.

Fear of being sexually inadequate can be particularly potent. But allow us to reassure you that eventually, when you succeed in establishing the lifestyle you are dreaming about, you will be so familiar with so many different individuals' ways of expressing sexuality that you will no longer have to wonder how your sexuality compares to another's; you'll know from direct experience. You can learn from your lovers, and your lovers' lovers, and your lovers' lovers' lovers, to be the sexual superstar you would like to be.

Unlearning Jealousy

To change the way you experience a feeling takes time, so expect a gradual process, learning as you go, by trial and error. And there will be trials, and you will make errors.

Start by giving yourself permission to learn new ways. Allow yourself to not know what you don't know, to be ignorant. You must allow yourself to make mistakes — you have no choice. So reassure yourself: there is no graceful way to unlearn jealousy. It's kind of like learning to skate — you have to fall down and make a fool of yourself a few times before you become as graceful as a swan.

The challenge becomes learning to establish within yourself a strong foundation of internal security that is not dependent on sexual exclusivity, or ownership of your partner. This is part of the larger question of how to grasp your personal power and learn to understand and love yourself without such a desperate need for another person to validate you. You become free to give and receive validation, not from need or obligation, but from love and caring. We suggest most strongly that you put some effort into learning to validate yourself — believe us, you're worth it.

Many people find that as they develop their polyamorous families, they actually get validation from lots and lots of people and thus become less dependent on their partner's approval. Their needs and their sources of nourishment get spread out over a wider territory.

We can't tell you how to banish jealousy, or how to exorcise it as if it were a demon. Jealousy is not a cancer that you can cut out. It is a part of you, a way that you express fear and hurt. What you can do is change the way you experience jealousy, learn to deal with it as you learn to deal with any emotion — until it becomes, not overwhelming and not exactly pleasant, but tolerable: a mild disturbance, like a rainy day rather than a typhoon.

DISEMPOWER YOUR JEALOUSY

One woman we talked to had some very good ideas about what you *can* do about jealousy:

I notice that jealousy comes and goes, depending on how good I feel about myself. When I'm not taking care of getting what I want, it's easy to get jealous and think that someone else is getting what I am not. I need to remember that it's my job to get my needs met. I feel the jealousy, but I'm not willing to act on it, so it mostly goes away.

Once you have made a commitment to refuse to act on your jealousy, you become free to start reducing the amount of power you let your jealousy have over you. One way to do this is simply by allowing yourself to feel it. Just feel it. It will hurt, and you will feel frightened and confused, but if you sit still, and listen to yourself with compassion and support for the scared child inside, the first thing you will learn is that the experience of jealousy is survivable. You have the strength to get through it.

We have heard sluts accuse each other of being jealous as if it were a crime: "See? Look at you! You're jealous, aren't you? Don't try to deny it!" It is particularly important that you own your jealousy, to yourself and to your intimates. If you try to pretend that you are not jealous when you are, others will perceive you as dishonest, or worse yet, they may believe you, and see no need to support or protect you because you're fine, right? If you pretend to *yourself* that you are not jealous when you are, then your own emotions may try devious routes to bring themselves to your attention, which can generate intensely irrational feelings and behavior, temper tantrums and hissy fits, or perhaps even make you physically ill.

When you deny your jealousy to yourself, you take from yourself the opportunity to be in sympathy with yourself and to support and comfort yourself. When you deny jealousy, or any other difficult emotion, you put yourself in a harsh and difficult landscape, full of pitfalls and land mines. "Acting out" means doing things you don't understand, driven by emotions you have refused to be aware of — and denying your jealousy can lead you to act out harsh feelings in ways you will regret later.

Sometimes acting out takes the form of making ultimatums about what your partner may and may not do — or, worse, trying to enforce retroactive "agreements" by getting all righteously indignant about how anybody could have figured out that it wasn't okay to take Bob to the movie *you* wanted to see, and aren't both of them inconsiderate and rotten? You cannot deal constructively with jealousy by making the other guys wrong. Jealousy is an emotion that arises inside you; no person and no behavior can "make" you jealous. Like it or not, the only person who can make that jealousy hurt less or go away is you.

Listening to your lover when she is feeling jealous can be difficult. Sometimes we find it easier to feel angry and push our beloved away than to stay close when she is in pain, to stay in empathy, to support, to care. When we blame a lover for being jealous, we are trying to justify our intense desire to not have to listen to how much he hurts when we are on the way out the door to play with someone else. This is a crummy way to avoid dealing with our own feelings of guilt.

If this sounds familiar to you, if you have experienced times like this in your life, we recommend that you practice the skill of staying quietly with both your own and your lovers' pain. Remember, you don't have to fix anything — all you have to do is listen, to yourself or another, and understand that this hurts. Period.

The way to unlearn jealousy is to be willing to experience it. By actively choosing to experience a painful feeling like jealousy, you are already starting to reduce its power over you. First, you decide that you will not allow your jealousy to make you run screaming over the horizon. And so you exercise your first form of control over jealousy: I will hold steady and stay with myself and my feelings.

Catherine and her partner had a difficult moment when she first told him that she was in love with one of her lovers.

I'd been seeing this woman for a while, and realized,
much to my surprise, that my feelings toward her had
gone beyond simple sexual friendship and into a deep

romantic emotion that I identified as being in love. When
I told Jay about this, I think his first impulse was to feel
threatened, insecure, and, yes, jealous. I could feel him
getting close to exploding. It was hard for me not to try
to fix things, to take back what I'd said about being in
love, or to simply leave the discussion altogether because
I felt scared and guilty.

But Jay stayed on course, allowing the feelings to
present themselves, but not allowing them to drive him
into acting angry or defensive. He asked me some
questions about what exactly this meant to us, and I was
able to explain that I wasn't planning to leave him, that
my love for her was in no way a threat to my love for
him, that she and I weren't expecting to become primary
partners — that, really, nothing had changed except my
own emotions and the words I was using to describe
them. We still re-visit this discussion from time to time,
especially when our busy schedules permit me to spend
some extra time with my lover. And, so far, we've all
been able to recognize and honor one another's
emotions, and things are going great.

You can feel jealousy without acting on it. In fact, flying into a
rage and breaking all the crockery, or calling your lover's lover and
hanging up every fifteen minutes during your first sleepless night, or
picking a fight with whoever's handy — all these are things that people
do in order to not feel jealous, in order to not feel scared and small.

When you hold still with your jealousy, you will find that it is
possible to feel something difficult without getting frantic, or doing

anything you don't choose to do. You will have taken your second step at disempowering your jealousy. You've told your jealousy that you will not allow it to destroy your loving relationships.

Your pain is the breaking of the shell that encloses your understanding.

Even as the stone of the fruit must break, that its heart may stand in the sun, so must you know pain.

And could you keep your heart in wonder at the daily miracles of your life, your pain would not seem less wondrous than your joy:

And you would accept the seasons of your heart, even as you have always accepted the seasons that pass over your fields. And you would watch with serenity through the winters of your grief.[11]

Weathering the Storm

So here you are, holding still, feeling rotten. Now what do you do? Get as comfortable as you can and listen to yourself. Explore your feelings, nourish them, treasure them — they are the most essential part of you.

Be good to yourself, and remember that the most important part of love is not the love, however wonderful, that you or another can have for your beauty and strength and virtue. The real test of love is when a person — including you — can know your weaknesses, your stupidities and your smallnesses, and still love you.

Remember, as you look at yourself, to look kindly, and also remember that you are not balancing a checkbook. Anything you see that you don't like, or that you want to change, is not a debit that you subtract from your virtues. Learn to reflect on your strengths and virtues, and it becomes easier to look constructively at your weaknesses. Keep your virtues at their full value, and cherish them.

Start by setting yourself the task of getting through a short period of time with your jealousy, like an evening or an afternoon when your partner may be off with another. Make a pact with yourself that you will stay with your feelings, whatever they may be, for a short period of time. If a whole evening or night seems like too long, start with five or ten minutes, then arrange to distract yourself with a video or whatever.

IT MIGHT BE EASIER THAN YOU THOUGHT

One of the possible, and indeed common, outcomes will be that your partner will go off on a date with another, and you will feel just fine. Surprise! Your anticipation may have been a lot worse than the actual event. Experienced sluts often find that they only feel jealous now and then. When they do experience jealousy, they can examine these specific experiences to see what they can learn about themselves, and if they can think of what might make this particular sort of event safer and easier.

One couple we talked to is working to maintain their primary relationship in a difficult situation: one of them is out of town most of the time on business, and thus much of their activity with other partners takes place under circumstances that prevent them from re-connecting physically to the primary relationship afterwards. One of their agreements is that they talk on the phone every single night, regardless of where they are or how busy they are. Often, their conversations take place after one of them has spent time connecting with an outside partner. One of them notes that during these conversations,

>...he allows my feelings. I don't hesitate to say
>anything I want; in fact, he encourages me to. I've found

*that just being allowed to say these things, to talk about
my jealousy and sadness, somehow defuses them. They
lose a lot of their power because they meet no resistance
from him — he just listens to them and lets them be.*

FEEL YOUR FEELINGS

Painful feelings, even the most intense of them, have a tendency to run
their course if you let them, so an initial strategy is to make yourself as
comfortable as possible and wait till the feelings die down. Find your
feelings, jealousy or hurt or anger or whatever, and let them flow through
you, like a river. Your mind may be racing with nasty thoughts, angry,
blaming, focusing on some detail that you're absolutely certain those
other people did wrong, obsessing on believing that someone is taking
advantage of you, or riding roughshod over your feelings. This hurts a
lot, so surely it must be somebody's *fault!* Allow us to reassure you: you
are not an idiot. We all go through this. Don't die of shame, just let these
thoughts run through you too.

Feelings, once uncovered, can be better understood by reflecting
on them. It is useful to have scripts and strategies for self-exploration.
Journal writing, preferably with total disregard for grammar and syntax,
can be a good way to vent feelings and learn about yourself at the same
time. It is okay to cover pages of your journal with FUCK FUCK FUCK
FUCK FUCK I HATE THIS! in bright red ink; if this feels good to you we
recommend you get a large size journal. Try writing down your stream
of consciousness, which means whatever you find in your head whether
or not it makes sense, and see what you get. Treasures, jewels of self-
knowledge, are often found here.

You can get a big drawing pad and a set of oil pastels, which are crayons for grownups. These big crayons encourage expression with bright colors, and discourage getting hung up on details (they're too fat to get crabby with). Sometimes you will draw, and get squiggles, and that's great — the smallest thing you can accomplish still helps you hold still for a while, and rant in color. Other times, you may surprise yourself with a drawing that is profoundly meaningful to you. Both of us use drawing a lot to vent our strong feelings and discover things about ourselves — Dossie quit smoking this way, and Catherine used it as an important tool to get out of suburbia and recover her sluthood — and we assure you that neither of us is a great artist.

Some people like to express their feelings with their bodies, and might like to run, or work out at the gym, or clean the kitchen, or dig in the garden. Try finding music that fits your mood, angry or sad or frantic, and dancing your feelings out. When you express yourself, you get to know yourself better and work out some of the most intense stress constructively. The least you could wind up with would be a clean kitchen, and you might actually feel good after a self-indulgent afternoon on the beach.

Poor baby

Try focusing on the feelings in your body: where do you feel these emotions, in your throat, chest, gut? Turning your attention to the physical sensations can intensify them, and might bring up tears, but they will move on through even more readily if you allow yourself to feel them on the physical level. If rage comes welling up, you can pound on a pillow. If you start to cry, let it flow, remembering the sense of relief that comes after expressing intense emotion in tears. Catherine likes to seek out a tear-jerker book or movie to help her get tears out when she feels stuck. ("Terms of Endearment" has never failed her yet.)

Some people have trouble doing this because they've been taught that it's wrong to feel sorry for yourself. So who else should you feel sorry for? Stay in sympathy with yourself: you feel bad, so be kind to yourself.

You can talk to a friend, or your other lover, presuming you have made agreements about confidentiality with everybody who might care if you gossip. Catherine has a deal with a good friend of hers for telephone support. She can call her friend up and ask for five minutes of "poor baby," and if her friend is available, she pours out her feelings and her friend says, you guessed it, nothing but "poor baby" till she is through. This may sound silly, but don't knock it till you try it. Comfort is a good thing in hard times.

WHO'S TO BLAME?

As you get skilled at finding and expressing your feelings, you can try a more challenging task — see if you can write about or talk to your friend about your feelings without blaming anybody — not your lover, not his lover, and especially not yourself. This is not an easy exercise: you will be surprised how readily we all slip into that blaming mode, but it is very very worthwhile to learn to have your feelings without foisting them off onto someone else's account.

Remember, it might be easier in the short run for me to dump my feelings on you — when I feel bad, it sure is tempting to make how I feel all your fault. But when we blame others for feelings that truly belong to us, we disempower ourselves. If it's your fault that I feel bad, I guess there's nothing I can do about it, so I'm stuck. Only when I am willing to own my emotions do I have the power to change and grow.

ONE TINY STEP IN THE DIRECTION OF...

When your emotions are overwhelming and chaotic, it can help to ask yourself if there is anything that would help you feel just one tiny bit safer. Let go of the big picture — maybe it's too big to figure the whole thing out right now, so start by taking a tiny step in the direction of safer. A few deep breaths, conscious relaxation of some muscles, soothing music — try wrapping yourself in a soft blanket. It may not seem like much, but once you manage to do anything that improves your lot even the littlest bit, you are moving in the right direction to build some confidence that you can learn to deal with your jealous feelings.

BABY YOURSELF

Give yourself permission to take good care of yourself while you learn to work through jealousy and other hard feelings. Learn to nurture yourself. What are the things you find comforting? Give them to yourself. Hot chocolate? Warm towels after a long soak? A long session with your most beloved movie or computer game? Your favorite teddy bear? Effective self-nurturing often happens on the level of body awareness, so nice physical experiences — massages, bubble baths, skin lotion, flannel nighties — can give a sense of comfort and security even when your mind is anxious and your thoughts are a mess. Give yourself permission to take the best possible care of yourself. You deserve it.

When you anticipate feeling jealous, make plans to occupy your time. It may be too much too ask that you always have a hot date at exactly the same time as your lover — most people's schedules are too complicated, and what do you do when one of your dates comes down with the flu? Do you cancel the other one? The people you make these dates with might be counting on you, the time they have with you might be important to them, their feelings might get hurt. Third parties have a right to some predictability in their lives too.

But even if you can't round up a hot date for yourself, you can probably find a friend to go to a movie with, rent a video, talk obsessively on the 'Net, grind your teeth, eat sugar, chew your fingernails, whatever works. We do not recommend drinking and drugging, as getting high might very well increase the intensity of your disturbance, and disinhibit you enough that you might forget your commitment to experience your jealousy without acting on it. Besides, although a certain amount of escapism is fine, to anesthetize yourself so that you feel nothing at all will never give you the opportunity to develop skills at dealing with all the feelings you have that are inspired by jealousy.

BITE THE BULLET

When no better plan is available, there is nothing wrong with gritting your teeth, biting the bullet and hanging in there till it's over. For now. Dossie remembers her first challenge after she decided to never be monogamous again:

> I had been casually dating a young man, and had told him at great length that I was not available for partnering, and had no intention of ever being monogamous again. He came over to visit at my home when my best friend was there, we all got a little stoned, and he came on to her. She thought he was neat, and didn't know I was involved with him, so they started necking right in the middle of my living room. Eeeek! My

thoughts went racing as I watched them, thinking — well, it's not like I want to marry him, and I don't think I feel like joining them, and I don't think my friend is bisexual anyway, so what do I do? Amy Vanderbilt has said nothing on the appropriate etiquette for this situation. For a while I sat doing nothing, frozen, to tell the truth, and finally I thought to myself, Okay, so there's no script, I'll have to make one up. What would I be doing if my friend and my new lover weren't rolling around on the floor with their braces locked? I guessed I'd be finishing taking the notes from that Tarot book I'm reading, so I went upstairs and studied, gritting my teeth, but focusing on my notes gave me at least a little relief by occupying my mind. Eventually they left, and I got through a strange and lonely night, not feeling necessarily great, but at least proud of myself that I had survived. I was particularly proud that I hadn't thrown my soup at them. I felt not at all damaged, really okay. Later I got to talk to my friend: our friendship survived, the dating relationship did not, which was fine by me. What I got a grip on was my own strength, so funky as it was, this was my first successful run through jealousy.

GO FOR THE ICK

A good question to ask yourself as you seek to understand your jealousy is, "What are the specific images that disturb me the most?" Chances are you are already imagining along these lines, so you're not likely to make yourself feel worse by thinking about the scary stuff on purpose.

Those disturbing images, the ones that really bother you, are not telling you what your partner is doing. You actually don't know what your partner is doing. The images you see in your mind are the perfect reflection of your own fears. One way to come to terms with your fears is to acknowledge them: "Yes, I'm afraid of that." You can take it even further, and work through the fears by envisioning the worst possible scenario that you can imagine. Go ahead, wallow in it. Elaborate it until it becomes ridiculous. Maybe that other guy has a dick three miles long, that girl is a perfect replica of a living Barbie doll. Maybe you can laugh at your fears: that'll take the power out of them.

Pay attention also to your imaginings that are less dangerous, less anxiety-ridden. This is where you feel safer. You may be surprised to find that imagining your lover in the midst of sex with someone else is less scary than you thought it would be, or maybe images of kissing bother you more than intercourse, or whatever. Try writing down your imaginings on index cards, then putting them in order from the most to the least scary. Then you will know what parts scare you the most, and what the safer-feeling parts are. Now you have a direction to turn your mind that will help you feel a little bit safer, which is your first step on the road to becoming perfectly comfortable.

Reality is less terrifying than fiction. You can counter your fears with reality testing. Our minds, like nature, abhor a vacuum. We get nervous. Think of the last time you were waiting for someone to return a call, or a family member was significantly late coming home. It may reassure you to know that the Highway Patrol is now computerized, and ready to deal with all of us who call and want to know if our beloved Joe Blow had an accident between there and here. We all do this. Catherine and her partner have an agreement to call each other before they leave a lover's house for the trip home, just to help prevent this kind of worry.

When we don't know what's going on, few of us are able to just say "I don't know" and stop thinking about it. We fill in the blanks, and in order to do that we make something up. What you see when you fill in the blanks has nothing to do with reality — what you see is your own worst fear. So now you know what you are afraid of, and nothing about what is really happening.

This is why your authors are biased in favor of full disclosure in free love. We are particularly in favor of multiple partners having a chance to meet each other, or at least hear about each other, to dispel our self-created mythology that that other person is younger, thinner, sexier, etc. You might be surprised, when you meet your lover's lover, to find the experience downright reassuring. The truth is that different individuals are apples and oranges, each with faults and virtues, and each one unique, which is why we like to relate to lots of them in the first place. Difference is wonderful, and remind yourself: this is not a contest, this is not a race. We all get to win.

REMEMBER THE GOOD STUFF

Make a list of everything you value about your relationship, and put it aside for a rainy day. Be an optimist, turn your mind to the positive end of things. Value what you have, and what you get from your partner; the time, attention and love that he shares with you, the good stuff that fills your cup. Avoid being the pessimist who focuses on what is not there, the energy that goes somewhere else. That energy is not subtracted from what you get — relationships are not balanced like checkbooks. So when you are feeling deprived, remember all the good stuff you get from your partnership.

SHARING

You and your partners need to practice talking about jealousy. When you try to pretend that you're so perfectly enlightened that you never feel jealous, you deprive yourself of the opportunity to work with your feelings and share support with your partner. And when you try to protect yourself and your partner from jealousy, you are engaging in a deception that can only lead to more distance, and can never bring you closer.

A couple we know tell us that they have developed a convention in their relationship that each can ask the other for what they call a "jelly moment." In your jelly moment, you get to say what's bothering you, that you feel scared and jealous, nervous about saying goodbye for the weekend, small and silly and your knees are feeling like, well, jelly. The other partner's commitment is to listen, sympathize and validate. That's the response — not "Okay, I'll cancel my date with Blanche," but "Aw, honey, I'm sorry you feel bad. I love you."

When we tell our partners that we feel jealous, we are making ourselves vulnerable in a very profound way. When our partners respond with respect, listen to us, validate our feelings, support and reassure us, we feel better taken care of than we would have if no difficulty had arisen in the first place. So we strongly recommend that you and your partners give each other the profoundly bonding experience of sharing your vulnerabilities. We are all human, we are all vulnerable, and we all need validation.

REPERTORY DRAMA

Your strategies for surviving periods of jealousy will stand you in good stead for the rest of your life, and you will use what you learn about yourself from this practice over and over. All of the techniques listed above are applicable to other difficult feelings, so now you not only have a repertoire of ways to deal with bouts of jealousy, but also to handle whatever other painful emotions may come your way. So when you get this far, congratulate yourself. Celebrate your successes: write "I am a genius!" two hundred times with lots of bright colors. Buy yourself something nifty. You've done a lot of hard work, and you deserve a reward.

A FINAL NOTE ABOUT LOVE

One remedy for the fear of not being loved is to remember how good it feels to love someone. If you're feeling unloved and you want to feel better, go love someone, and see what happens.

CHAPTER 4. SLUTS IN LOVE

We hear too often of folks who enjoy a joyously slutty lifestyle until they fall in love. Then, perhaps prodded by cultural messages that love must equal marriage must equal monogamy, they suddenly skydive into an attempt at a conventional lifestyle, often with disastrous consequences. At least one of your authors — you can insert Catherine's rueful grin here — is not immune to this kind of programming.

There is no reason why wedding bells, or the equivalent thereof, need to break up that old gang of yours. Many sluts find it possible to combine the committed stability of a life partnership with the multifarious pleasures of sex and intimacy with others.

However, there is no question that being a slut within a committed relationship has some special challenges. So much of our cultural baggage tells us that commitment equals ownership — that, as the old bitter joke has it, a ring around the finger equals a ring through the nose. Even people who know better often find that their expectations of a committed relationship may include the right to control many aspects of their partner's lives.

As you can probably guess, we don't much like the idea that a relationship commitment specifies anybody's right to anything beyond mutual respect and caring for each other. Yet once you divorce romantic love from the concept of ownership, what happens? Dossie's partner, who has never been in an open relationship before, was startled to find that many of her old habits have become irrelevant: "Why should I bother to look for stray hairs or inconsistent stories, trying to sniff out any trace of infidelity, when I know that if she has sex with someone else she'll simply tell me about it?" Yet there *are* still issues of boundaries, of responsibility, of courtesy, that override the ownership issue, and must be dealt with.

So, how do two sluts in love (or more — we'll write this chapter based on a two-partner agreement for the sake of simplicity, but the issues involved come up in multipartner arrangements as well) build a life together?

Our friends Ruth and Edward remember: "We had a monogamous relationship for about sixteen years, then opened it up and started interacting with other people. Now we're trying to figure out what we're comfortable doing with other people, and what we want to reserve for our own relationship. Sometimes, the only way to locate the boundary of our comfort zone is to cross it and feel the discomfort. We try to take small steps, so that the pain is minimal. We're definitely committed to each other, and are each willing to stop doing things that the other finds threatening."

Mostly, you take care of your own stuff, recognize and protect your boundaries, and make agreements to help yourself and your partner feel safe — but we've already talked about that. Here are some special problems that may come up for partnered sluts.

THE ACCIDENTAL COUPLE

We've said before that each relationship seeks its own level. For some relationships, that's a life partnership, which may include sharing living space, possessions, and so on. Others may take other forms: occasional dates, friendships, ongoing romantic commitments, and so on. Yet many folks find that they've gotten into a habit of letting their relationships slide inexorably into life partnership, without much thought or intent on their part. Well-meaning friends and acquaintances may aid in this process by assuming that you and your friend are a couple before you've ever decided to become one. In addition, many people get coupled by accident, by virtue of an unplanned pregnancy, an "eviction romance" where one partner loses a housing situation and moves in with the other, or simple convenience. Catherine remembers:

> In my freshman year of college, I met a guy I liked a lot — quiet and shy, but when he said anything I really liked what he had to say. Fred and I wound up going out together a couple of times, and having sex a few times. When school ended, we wrote to each other over the summer. Then fall came and I began looking around for a place to live outside the dorms. The only room I could find was a double-sized room which I could only afford if I shared it with someone. So I called Fred and proposed that we share it, putting up a partition across the middle and sleeping on separate mattresses, and he agreed.
>
> The first night there, Fred had already gotten himself a mattress, and I hadn't yet — so I shared his. Somehow, we never did get around to getting another mattress. We wound up living together for a couple of years, then getting married. That missing mattress led to a fifteen-year marriage and a couple of kids.

While we're all for coupledom for people who choose it, we like to see folks make their choices a bit more mindfully than this. We suggest that before you let yourself slide into something that you don't really want, you do some serious thinking and talking, alone and together, about what is the best form for this particular relationship. Talk to each other about what love means to you, and how you fit into each other's lives.

You may discover that while you enjoy one another's company and have fabulous sex, your habits regarding housing, money, possessions and so on are wildly incompatible. In such a situation, you could do what generations of people have done — move in together and spend years trying to change one another, getting frustrated and resentful in the process. Or you could reconsider some of the implicit assumptions you have brought to the relationship. Do you have to live together? Why? Why not instead enjoy your friend for the things you like about him, and find someone else with which to share the other things? Sluthood means, among other things, that you don't have to depend on any one person to fulfill all your desires.

If you know that you're a person who tends to slide into coupledom, we suggest spending some serious time trying to figure out why you've fallen into this pattern and what you hope to get out of being a couple. It's a very good idea for everyone to learn to live single — to figure out how to get your needs met without being partnered, so you don't find yourself seeking a partner to fill needs that you ought to fill yourself. You might also consider experimenting with some relation-ships unlike those you've tried in the past — instead of looking for Mr. or Ms. Right, try dating some people you like and trust but don't necessarily love, or maybe love in a quieter way than chills running up your spine.

In this, as in just about everything else we've told you in this book, the key is to build your own sense of internal security. If you like yourself, love yourself, and take care of yourself, your other relationships can arrange themselves around you, as perfectly as crystals. We hope that if and when you get coupled, you do it on purpose.

SLUTS IN COMPETITION

One problem that often arises between partners is competition to be the most popular, a concern most of us have carried around in the bottom of our psyches since junior high school. Sometimes partners compete with each other, to see who can score the most, or the most attractive of conquests — an ugly picture.

We cannot reiterate often enough: this is not a contest, this is not a race, and no one is the prize. One strategy to cut through any feelings of competitiveness is to play matchmaker for each other, to invest yourself in your partner's sexual happiness as you do in your own. Remember the climax of "The Big Chill," in which a woman character sets up her best friend with her husband so that the friend could have a baby? Catherine recalls meeting a new Internet acquaintance for coffee, and hearing her describe a pet sexual fantasy that was startlingly similar to Catherine's partner's — Catherine set up their first date for later that week.

Dossie remembers being out with a long-time lover of hers when she noticed an attractive person trying to catch her eye behind her date's back. As they were leaving, Dossie explained this to her friend, who had a stroke of genius. He strode over the young man in question, and with great dignity announced, "My lady would like you to have her phone number." Dossie has made use of this strategy repeatedly since then, and recommends it highly: they always call!

CRUSHES

We have pointed out before that it is impossible for anyone to predict what depth of feeling may potentially exist in any sexual relationship. Many people new to open relationships try to limit outside sexual encounters to a casual, recreational level to avoid the terrifying specter of seeing your partner in love with, or at least crushed out on, another. And it is true that sometimes an outside relationship will threaten to become primary and supplant the existing partner, and when this happens everyone involved will feel horrible, particularly the person who may lose his partnership. Especially when that person has struggled to own their jealousy, and worked hard on his fears of abandonment, only to find himself actually abandoned and left out in the cold.

It is not possible to predict when or with whom a crush, or any other deepening of feelings, might happen. We certainly do not want to draw the boundaries of our agreements so tightly that we exclude everybody we like. There is no rule that will protect us from our own emotions, so we need to look beyond rules for solutions and for a sense of security.

It can help to do a reality check on your fantasies and expectations. New relationships are often exciting because they *are* new, glowing with sexual arousal, and too new to have uncovered the inevitable conflicts and disturbances that come with true intimacy over time. Every relationship has a honeymoon phase, and it is a true, if tragic, fact of life that the honeymoon cannot last forever. When we refuse to figure this out, we can wind up flying from partner to partner, always imagining that the next partner will be the perfect one. We may never stay with anyone long enough to discover the deeper intimacy and profound security that comes with confronting, struggling with, and conquering the hard parts of intimacy together.

Our friend Carol wisely notes:

Sexual time is connected with intimate time for most of us; we come to depend on our partners for various kinds of emotional support. So we get into this pattern where we share all our hard emotional un-sexy needs — all the work of living together, the sickness and health, richer and poorer stuff — with our life partner, and we're on our "best behavior" with our other partners. It can be important to remember that, while you may be trading away some of that juicy excitement of a brand-new unknown partner, the intimacy you get in return is valuable too, and you can't have that with a person you met two weeks ago. The trick is to find a way to manifest both possibilities — the intimacy of sharing and the heat of novelty — in your own life.

Remember, please, that fantasy is not reality, and enjoy your fantasies while you maintain your commitments. When your expectation is that a crush is a brief, if wonderful, experience, you and your partner can live through one with relative equanimity, and more important, without destroying your long term stability and love with each other.

RELATING TO THIRD PARTIES

Your relationship with your lover's lovers brings up points of etiquette that Miss Manners never dreamed of. One couple we talked to noted,

"It's important that we not be totally grossed out or disgusted by one another's lovers — especially if it's going to be long term, it helps if we can all be friends."

Dossie has a story to tell about this.

I was once in a relationship with a man who had a primary partner whom I had not met. I had asked to meet her, and she was considering if she felt safe enough to do that. Their arrangement was that when Patrick had a date with me, Louisa would make a date with her other lover, and everybody would, hopefully, feel safe and taken care of. Unfortunately, Louisa's other lover frequently stood her up, and then Patrick would stand me up, which I began to find unacceptable. This was the first time I had asserted any right to consideration of me as the outside lover — we are so used to seeing the outsider as the homewrecker that we rarely think to protect that person's feelings. With much back and forth, and the promised meeting, Louisa finally agreed that Patrick could see me whether or not she had a date, and we would make sure that she got plenty of advance notice, that he got home on time, and that she got lots of support from both of us. As we worked through this, Louisa and I got closer and closer — I particularly remember one night when we were worried about Patrick, and sat up late talking about him while he slept in the next room. Louisa and I became best friends and went into business together, putting on workshops and theater presentations. We all three traveled together, and had a wonderful time.

Patrick and I wound up growing apart as lovers, but the friendship between me and Louisa carried on. What was important for me is that when we allowed ourselves to determine what boundaries fit for us at any given time, that freed us up to evolve through a series of changing relationships that made us close family for many years.

Should you meet the "third party"? We vote yes: if you don't, you'll almost certainly wind up imagining someone cuter, sexier, more predatory and more threatening than anyone could be outside a Hollywood erotic thriller. Besides, who knows? — you might wind up liking him. Some of our best friends are people we met because someone we were fucking was fucking them too. Catherine and her partner's commitment ceremony was performed by a priestess who had first been a lover of her partner's, and later a lover and close friend of Catherine's.

If you are gay or bisexual, you may, as Catherine did, find yourself considering forming a liaison with this person yourself — we talked to one woman whose first experience with open relationships took place when her girlfriend was fucking another woman, and our friend wound up falling in love with the other woman. ("My girlfriend got kind of cranky about this," she remembers wryly. "We're all tight family now, but it took a decade to get here.") We suggest a few moments of soul-searching to make sure your motivation is loving or lustful rather than vengeful or competitive — then, if you "test clean," go for it. It's really not too surprising that you like the same people your partner likes, and mutual attractions like these can form the nucleus of a long-lasting and very rewarding little tribe.

On the other hand, we sometimes see sluts who feel like they *have* to be sexual with their lover's lovers. In some cases, both parties in a partnership have an agreement only to play with a third party together. Such agreements require that both partners have "veto power" over potential thirds — being sexual with someone who you find unattractive or unpleasant is a very bad idea for you and for them. On the other hand, basic slut ethics should not allow you to abuse this power to prevent your partner from having sex with anyone at all by vetoing everybody: a strategy which may seem tempting, because until you unlearn jealousy, all outside engagements can look very threatening. Sometimes you need to gather up your strength, face down your fears, and unlearn by doing.

Or you may simply feel that since your partner likes and lusts after this person so much, you should too — to assuage your partner's guilt, to confirm her excellent taste, or to satisfy some obscure sense of fairness. Please don't. If you simply don't feel hot for this person, don't let yourself be driven into a position where you feel you have to fuck out of politeness: there are many other excellent ways for people to relate to one another. Cook her a nice dinner, go to the movies with her, play cards together, or find some other way to help her feel accepted into your life.

Which brings up an important question: how much responsibility do you have for helping your lover's lovers feel secure and welcome? Catherine has spent many long telephone conversations reassuring her partner's lovers that, yes, it's *really* okay with her, and have a great time, honey. We think that your own needs should be of primary importance to you, and if you really just can't be welcoming and supportive then you shouldn't. On the other hand, we also think it's gracious to be as friendly as you can without having to grit your teeth and force a smile. At minimum, we suggest that you at least try to provide some reassurance that this is not a competition, that you are not being harmed by anything that's going on, and that you are able to take care of your own emotions — in other words, a promise to own your own stuff and not blame the third party. After all, he's doing this because he feels the same way you do — that your partner is the hottest thing on legs — and not because he wants to destroy your life.

After the crush is over, some people will find a long term place in your life, often unexpected, like the lover who has become your kid's favorite uncle, or your partner's business partner. Others may leave, and when they leave with warm feelings, they may come back again in the future, when once again there is a place for them in your life, or for you in theirs. Thus the infinitely connected polyamorous slut builds his web of extended families and tribes. And we feel there is some truth in the notion that a family of lovers cannot fail.

Some very capable sluts maintain more than one primary relationship. Dossie has known one such couple, Robert and Celia, for twenty-five years. They have been married twenty-four years, and have together raised two children from previous relationships. Each has another primary partner, both usually women, and family relationships with all their exes. Robert's outside partner May was originally lover to Celia's lover Judy back in 1985, then became lovers with Celia, and finally with Robert from 1988 to the present, and, they intend, on into the future. Some years ago Miranda and Celia lived upstairs, and Robert and May lived downstairs. Currently Cheryl, another of Celia's previous girlfriends, lives upstairs and helps with the grandchildren; Miranda, another of Celia's exes, visits two days a week since she lives out of town but attends school nearby. All of these people, plus many other friends and lovers of various degrees of intimacy, both present and historical, and most of *their* friends and lovers, form a very long-term extended family that has lived, loved and raised children together for almost thirty years, and plan to care for one another in their old age. We are impressed.

The Ebb and Flow of Relationships

We observe, with much delight, the number of our old lovers we count among our present friends, and how sexual relationships can develop into family memberships. There is a reality limit here — you only have twenty-four hours a day to devote to your love life, and presumably you need some of those hours for work and sleep and so on, so you have a finite amount of time to devote to each of your lovers. You can only fit a certain number of people in your life and expect to do any of them justice.

We find that most people do okay letting their partners come and go as it feels right for each of them. Extended family sexual relationships are more likely to grow apart than to break up. One of the very wonderful things about building sexual friendships is that, while past relationships and smaller affairs may come and go over the years, each pairing has its own characteristic and unique intimacy. You create this intimacy the way you learn to ride a bike — by trial and error, slipping and falling, and ultimately zooming along together. Just like riding a bike, you'll never forget this particular intimacy, or your own role in it. Even after the most bitter of separations, when conflict is cleared and time has healed the wounds, you may find that you can slip that connection right back on, like a comfortable old glove.

TROUBLE IN PARADISE

On the other hand, sometimes conflict in an intimate relationship goes on so long, or seems so impossible to resolve, that it threatens the very foundation of that relationship. We hope you will bring the same high level of ethics and concern to a conflicted relationship that you brought to a happy one.

It is always tempting to respond to a major relationship conflict by assigning blame. In childhood we learn that pain, in the form of punishment from our all-powerful parents, is the consequence of doing something wrong. So when we hurt, we try to make sense of it by finding somebody doing something wrong, preferably somebody else. We have discussed the disempowerment of blaming before. What is important to remember is that most relationships break up because the partners are unhappy with each other, and no one is to blame: not you, not your partner, and not your partner's lover. Even if someone acted badly, or was dishonest, your primary relationship probably isn't falling apart for that reason — relationships tend to end due to their own internal stresses. Even your authors have trouble remembering this when we are in the middle of a bitter breakup.

When you find yourself blaming a lot, it may help to remember a truism of relationship counseling: the "client" is the relationship itself, not either of the people in it. If you start looking at conflicts, problems and so on as problems of the relationship, instead of trying to decide whose fault they are, you have taken an important first step in solving them.

Traditionally in this culture, women often bear the burden of being responsible for everybody's emotional well-being. A woman's inability to magically make pain and trouble disappear is rarely at the heart of a relationship conflict, although she may feel as guilty and inadequate as if it were. In this pattern, one partner takes too much responsibility for the problem, so it becomes important to distinguish what each partner's responsibilities are.

On the other hand, it's also common for one partner to take too little responsibility. Women (and sometimes men) who have a lot of their self-esteem connected to their ability to maintain a relationship may feel the need to make their partner into the "villain," in order to justify their own desire to leave. This strategy is unfair to both of you: it gives the "villain" all the power in the relationship, and disempowers the "victim": deciding that you have no choice but to leave because your partner is so horrible is denying the fact that there are always choices. Our experience is that relationship troubles are almost always two-sided: if you can acknowledge your own contribution to the problem, you can work toward solving it.

We should note here, however, that if your relationship problems include anybody being physically violent, or emotionally or verbally abusive, it's not time to waffle over whose fault it is — it's time to get professional help in learning to resolve conflict in a non-destructive manner. The Resource Guide in the back of this book will tell you how to get in touch with groups in your area that help both battered and battering partners.

Breaking up

It happens. Good relationship skills and high ethics don't mean you get to be with the same partner or partners forever and ever. It is our experience that relationships change, people grow out of them, people change. They may acquire new desires, new dreams. Some breakups

THE TEN GREAT LIES OF SLUTHOOD
(A TONGUE-IN-CHEEK GUIDE)

I NEVER GET JEALOUS.

FUCKING OTHER PEOPLE DOESN'T DIMINISH MY SEXUAL FREQUENCY WITH MY PRIMARY PARTNER.

I'D STOP THIS IF SHE REALLY WANTED ME TO.

I ALWAYS TELL THE COMPLETE TRUTH ABOUT MY OUTSIDE PARTNERS.

I'M NEVER TEMPTED TO LEAVE MY PRIMARY FOR ONE OF MY OTHER PARTNERS.

WE NEVER COMPETE FOR THE SAME PERSON.

NOBODY'S KEEPING SCORE HERE.

I DON'T MIND IF THEY USE OUR BED/OUR CAR/OUR SEX TOYS.

WE ALWAYS PLAN EVERYTHING IN ADVANCE.

THERE'S NOTHING TO BE UPSET ABOUT.

in our own lives, as we look back with 20-20 hindsight, were actually constructive moves toward personal growth and a healthier life for each of us. At the time, however, we just felt awful.

When a traditional marriage breaks up, nobody takes that as evidence that monogamy doesn't work — so why do people feel compelled to take a sluts' breakup as evidence that free love is impossible? Your breakup may be for reasons entirely unrelated to the openness of your relationship. At any rate, it probably isn't evidence that you aren't meant to be a slut: we suspect you wouldn't have done all the hard work it takes to live this way if you hadn't had a strong desire for sluthood in the first place.

It's important to remember that a breakup isn't necessarily the *end* of a relationship — it may be, instead, a shift to a different kind of relationship, possibly a relationship between courteous acquaintances, or friends, or maybe even lovers. One of the nice things about being an ethical slut is that your relationships become non-binary; you may have as many ways of relating to your friends and lovers as you have friends and lovers. Dossie remembers:

> *I dated Bill for such a long time — a year and a half — that by the time I announced to our friends that we were officially a couple, everybody laughed at me: big news, ha ha. We moved in together, and that lasted for all of six months before we blew up in a massive fight and separated. It was a year before we could be around each other much, but then we started having sex again, because our sex together had always been really hot. And we wound up getting together once a month or so for fully nine years as good friends, continuing to have*

*the same wonderful steamy sex that had brought us
together in the first place.*

When a relationship shifts dramatically, it's great if everybody
feels calm enough to separate with affection and equanimity. But all too
often, partnerships break up, divorce happens, in a harsh way, with
painful, angry, hurt and bitter feelings. Grief at losing a relationship
that we had counted on cuts deep, and while we are going through the
hurtful process of an unwelcome separation, none of us are at our best.

A typical grief process takes about three months to get past the
acute phase. What that means is that feelings of grief, loss, abandonment,
anger, resentment and what-have-you that are overwhelming or
intolerable today will probably seem sad but manageable three months
from now. A useful rule of thumb is that as the feelings die down, it's a
good time to get back into communication with your ex — have some
coffee or go to a movie or some such. It would be a shame not to come
out of this breakup with at least a friendship, after all you've shared.

Who gets the friends?

One of the joyous consequences of open sexual lifestyles is that
everybody tends to get interconnected in an extended family, sexual
circle or tribe. When a couple breaks up with lots of pain, then the
whole circle is affected. For the people in pain, it can feel like there is no
privacy. Your friends and other lovers may be full of their own ideas
about who done who wrong. It hurts them when they feel your pain, so
the entire circle may start looking for someone to blame.

Ethically speaking, the separating couple has some responsibility
toward their intimate circle, and the circle has some responsibility toward
the erstwhile couple. The members of the couple should refrain from

trying to split the community. This means you don't demand that all your friends sever whatever friendships they may have with your ex, and that you don't divide your community up into those who are on your side and those who are against you by virtue of who continues to speak to your unspeakable ex.

Privacy is a touchy issue here, because no one likes the consequences of gossip run amok — but we all need a confidant to tell our troubles to, especially in hard times. Sometimes separating couples can make agreements about who it's okay to talk about private matters with, and who we would rather not have familiarized with our dirty linen. Other times, no agreement is reached, and the chips fall where they may.

If you feel that you and your ex should not be at the same parties for a while, you need to work that out with each other, and not wind up screaming at your host for having invited both of you to the same event. It is particularly unethical to call up the host of a certain party and ask them to disinvite your ex, or blackmail them by telling them that you won't come if your ex is invited. This constitutes foisting your work off on your friends. It is your task to set your boundaries, to make agreements with your ex, and, if you find yourself feeling bad in any place where your ex is also socializing, then it is your decision whether to stay or leave. We recommend that you make your decision to stay or leave according to your own comfort, or discomfort, level, rather than trying to control someone else's behavior. And if you wind up deciding that you want to attend this event so much that you will just have to deal with your ex's presence, all to the better: you will get some practice at sharing social space with your ex, which you are going to need to do eventually unless one of you moves to Timbuktu. And eventually you *will* get good at dealing with your feelings about your ex, and with practice all of this will hurt less, and you will be closer to achieving resolution and even possibly friendship after a bitter breakup.

Your circle of friends and family is responsible for not getting split, for listening without judging, and for understanding that all of us think harsh thoughts while we are breaking up. Validate how bad your friend feels and take any condemnations with a grain of salt. The exception to this rule occurs when a breakup is based on the revelation of serious issues, like domestic violence or destructive substance abuse: there are no easy answers here, because a circle of sexual partners really does need to make judgments about these things. But most of the time, the accusations are about what a thoughtless, selfish, insensitive, bitchy, dishonest, manipulative, passive-aggressive, rude and stupid oaf that ex-partner is; we have all been all of these at some time or another, so we should be able to understand and forgive.

While breakups are very hard for all concerned, and while we understand that you may feel very angry, sad, abandoned, or ill-treated for a while, we implore you to remember that your soon-to-be-ex-partner is still the same terrific person you used to love, and to burn no bridges. Catherine says:

> *After our breakup, my ex-husband was very angry with me and pretty depressed, and I felt very guilty. Still, for the sake of the kids of whom we had joint custody, we made a point of staying on civil terms. Now, eight years later, I count him among my best friends: we still swap murder mysteries, share poetry, and talk on the phone for hours. If we'd been awful to one another back*

when things were raw and difficult, I don't think we'd be able to be on such good terms today, and we'd both have missed out on a very important and rewarding friendship.

CHAPTER 5. CONFLICT

Intimacy is based on shared vulnerability. Write this on your bathroom mirror. We'll never discount all the wonderful things that we get from sharing love, laughter, happiness and such, but nothing deepens intimacy like the experiences that we share when we feel flayed, with our skins off, scared and vulnerable, and our partner is there with us, willing to share in the scary stuff. These are the times that bring us the closest together.

WHAT'S IN IT FOR YOU?

Some people find it surprising to learn that a slut can experience overwhelming insecurities, but the truth is that sluts are just as nervous as anyone else, and skills to deal with our anxieties were not taught us in our cradles.

Your freedom might turn out to be a lot easier to accept than your partner's. It certainly does not follow that just because we can date others with equanimity that we will be equally calm when our partner does so. Going out and staying home are separate functions, like cooking and eating, each with its own rewards, and each requires specific skills to accomplish.

When problems arise, a good question to ask yourself is "What am I hoping to get out of this situation?" Why are you doing all this hard work to become a slut? The answer depends on your own individual situation, but for many of us, the payoff is our own freedom — and we have to learn to give freedom to our partners if we're going to get it for ourselves.

Fighting Fair

Thinking about how intimacy and bonding is cemented by sharing vulnerable feelings brings us to perhaps the ultimate act of intimacy: fighting. Many people believe that fighting between partners is to be avoided at all costs, but most relationship therapists would disagree. Fights between partners appear to be a universal experience; not many people actually enjoy them, but they seem to be necessary, a constructive element in the building of solid relationships. Only by fighting can partners struggle with their disagreements and express their most heartfelt feelings.

There has to be a way to communicate anger in a long-term relationship, and there has to be a way to struggle with disagreements. How many times have you had a bitter argument with your partner, and when it was over, felt closer than you had before?

So the problem, as we see it, is not to avoid fighting but to learn to fight in ways that are not destructive: physically, morally or emotionally. A good fight is very different from abuse — in a good clean fight, there is respect for safety and mutuality so that both people get to express their feelings at full volume, and come out the other end stronger and closer than before — bonded by fire, as it were.

The concept of "Fair Fighting" was first expounded by Dr. George R. Bach in his wonderful 1968 book, "The Intimate Enemy: How to Fight Fair in Love and Marriage." We strongly recommend that you read this book, even though it is dated and heterosexist, and even though the authors admit that they haven't even tried to conquer jealousy. They think jealousy is too hard for them — maybe they'll read *this* book. But the material on communication, and the detailed descriptions of how you can learn to share your anger with your partner in a constructive way, is priceless. This book is a classic.

WIN–WIN SOLUTIONS

A good fight starts with the understanding that in order for a fight to be successful, both people have to win. If one person wins a fight and the other loses, the problem causing the fight has not been resolved. It is naive to imagine that the person who "lost" has given up their interest in whatever issue is at stake. And when they feel overpowered, outgunned, or shouted down, they will be resentful, and the problem will go on being a problem. The only real way to win is to come to a solution where all parties concerned feel that they have won. So in a good clean fight, everybody's feelings get heard and considered, and solutions are decided on by agreement, not bullying.

We make a fight fair by agreeing on rules and limits, by respecting other people's right to their feelings and opinions while we are expressing our own. It is usually helpful to schedule a time to fight, and make an agreement to do so — it does not promote fair fighting if we waylay our partners in the bathroom when they are late for work. We need to schedule discussions at a time when we can give them our full attention.

Scheduling fights has the added advantage that we can prepare for them, organize our thoughts, and that we know we have a time when this particular issue will be dealt with. If I feel bad about the grocery bills on Tuesday, and I know we have a date to fight about it on

Thursday, it's pretty easy to put my stuff aside until then. Most people don't put their stuff aside very well when it seems that their issues will never get dealt with.

Whaddaya mean, schedule a fight? Don't they just erupt, like volcanoes? And when we have a fight, we are not likely to obey any rules or respect any limits, right? Aren't we talking about intense emotional outbursts? Well, yes, we are, but we don't believe that you can settle any issues when you are in an intense emotional state. When your feelings erupt, it is important to acknowledge them and pay attention. However awkwardly you may be expressing yourself, this is your truth; you obviously feel strongly about it, so it's an important truth. That's what we learn from our outbursts.

So while you are bursting out is a time to listen to your own truth. If emotions are being expressed at such a level of intensity that things feel out of control, like pounding on the walls or screaming at the top of your lungs, then it's time to take time out and land yourself. Either person can call for a "time out," which means that both people agree that they will take certain actions: perhaps be in separate rooms for a while, or take separate walks, or whatever will make it possible for you to quiet down and listen to your own feelings. A time out is not a time to try and listen to your partner: you will do that later. It may be difficult to cut yourself off in mid-rant, and you may feel abandoned if your partner reduces her anger by taking a walk — but sometimes this rough transition is the best way for each of you to own how you feel, and not let a fight escalate in a direction you both know from experience will be destructive. It will be much easier to talk about whatever it is when you are both feeling more serene.

Following is an agenda for a fair fight that Dossie uses with couples in her practice. If you want to try this out, pick a small issue, like how does the toilet get cleaned, and run through these steps.

EVERYBODY-WINS STEPS TO NO-LOSE CONFLICT RESOLUTION[13]

1.   Take TIME OUT to ventilate anger.

2.   Select ONE issue to work on.

3.   Make an APPOINTMENT to talk.

4.   Each person gets three minutes to state HOW I FEEL. Hint: Use I-statements, avoid YOU-messages, consider allowing time between each person's statement. Listen carefully.

5.   BRAINSTORM: write a list of ALL possible solutions, even silly ones.

6.   EDIT the list: cross out any suggestions that either person feels they could not live with.

7.   CHOOSE a solution to try for a specific period of time.

8.   RE-EVALUATE when that time is up.

I-MESSAGES

Notice that communication begins with everybody talking about their feelings, long before they get to discussing the pros and cons of any solutions. Good communication is based on identifying our feelings, communicating them to our partners, and getting validation from our partners that they hear and understand what we are saying. This is best done in sentences that begin with "I feel." There is an enormous difference between saying "you are making me feel so bad," and "I feel so bad." The second statement, the I-message, is a pure statement of feeling, and there is no accusation in it. So your lover doesn't feel attacked, and doesn't need to defend herself, but is free to actually listen to you. Conversely, sentences beginning with "you," and particularly "you always," usually are perceived as attacks, and responded to with defensiveness.

Most of us resent it when another person tells us how we feel — whether or not they are correct is immaterial. It is a violation of our boundaries when another person tells us what our inner truth is. Dossie trained with a supervising therapist who used to point his finger at clients and say, "I know what your problem is!" You probably already know how you feel when someone does that to you.

We can't ask our lover to hold still while we sling accusations and use her as a target for our frustrations. That would be asking her to consent to being abused, and she would be right to resist. But we can ask her to listen to how we feel, because putting aside her own agenda for a few minutes and listening to our feelings is a do-able task for the listener.

To learn how to use I-messages, try talking about an issue that is current for you without ever using the word "you," and without talking about what anyone else is doing, but only about your own feelings. This takes a little practice, but is less difficult than it may seem at first.

And when we listen to our lovers telling us how they feel, we can really hear. We learn how the world looks from their shoes, we can appreciate how they feel, we can validate their position. And then the solutions flow so much freer and more naturally. There are no wrong solutions, and no right ones — only the answers that fit well with how we all feel.

Differing Goals

What if it comes to pass, as it sometimes does, that after some exploration you and your partner discover that one of you wants an open relationship and the other one does not? Your authors strongly encourage you not to enter into a mortgage until you get this one straight, but you may discover this truth about yourselves after you've already bought a house and had triplets, so what then? When this difference is discovered after a relationship has been developed over a period of years, divorce is not an easy answer.

And perhaps you are a slut who loves your partner, and earnestly does not want to leave your home and your children to pursue the joys of sluthood. You can use all the strategies included here to try and work through your differences, and make agreements you can both live with. This is probably the most difficult and painful circumstance that can arise, and many relationships do not survive it.

Some couples do manage to stay together and develop enough openness to satisfy the one, and enough exclusivity to satisfy the other. They can get renewed commitment and intimacy from their struggles with these issues. Perhaps the less explorative partner can learn that his partner's exploration is not truly dangerous to him or to his relationship, and perhaps the explorative partner can learn to make changes slowly, or to accept some limits to her field of exploration because she genuinely cares about her partner's feelings. Over time, perhaps the mismatched pair will come closer to each other, if not in behavior, at least in acceptance.

Dossie relates:

I fell in love at the tender age of fifty with a woman my age who was a novice at nonmonogamy. She decided she was willing, and that our relationship is important enough for her to work on these issues, and I decided that I valued our relationship enough to set some limits to my own outrageousness, out of respect for my lover's feelings and to give her a chance to learn the freedom I have developed over twenty-seven years of free loving. Some might think we were ill-advised to enter into a committed relationship with such a huge difference in our experience, but we are totally crazy about each other, and this partnership is worth the earth to me — I am willing to do whatever work is necessary to make this work for both of us, and I know she is too.

Some things have been easy — group sex, for instance, has never bothered her, and we go to parties together and have dates with our friends with no difficulty. Our agreement is that when we go to group sex environments, we will discuss our plans beforehand, and we rarely engage in any activity that does not include the other, although we well may in the future.

My lover has more problems when I go on dates with another person on an individual basis, and so we are working on that, very slowly, to give her time to work through her feelings, and me mine, as we related earlier in this book.

Recently, a new wrinkle occurred when a friend asked my partner for a date. My lover decided that she wasn't ready to make dates with others because it feels too much like cheating on me, but she is comfortable with playing individually with this woman at a party, so she will probably do that. This is an example of how you can respect your own limits. Our friend was careful to ask me how I felt about her propositioning my lover, and so I feel respected and cared for as well. We don't know how exactly this will look a year from now, but for the present we love our relationship, we love our friends and lovers, and we love each other and plan to grow older, and sexier, together.

HELP IS AVAILABLE

You don't have to do all this on your own. Many wonderful books, classes and workshops are available — we've listed a few good ones in the back of this book. It's a good idea to put aside some time and energy to learn about communication, and to do it *with* the person you're trying to communicate with. There are many wonderful weekend workshops focusing on communication for couples; even your local church may well offer a weekend marriage retreat. We've never known a couple who went to a communication or intimacy workshop and didn't gain some good new skills and insights from it. Some workshops exist specifically to work on issues arising from nonmonogamy. We encourage you to take them, or to join a support group suitable to your needs. Just knowing that others struggle with some of the same issues that you do can help.

A somewhat more expensive, but still excellent, option is to do some sessions with a couples counselor. In general, we recommend this as a second-level alternative, after you've already done some classes and workshops, unless you have privacy concerns that make classes and workshops difficult for you.

Screen any of these resources about whether they'll be accepting of your open relationship. Some old-fashioned psychologists, and some workshops and retreats, may believe that your lust for many people is a "symptom" of psychological disturbance in you — you may not feel adequately safe and supported in such an environment. If you need help finding a sympathetic therapist or group, try asking your friends, or checking the Resource Guide in this book.

We strongly recommend that you investigate these types of help sooner rather than later. Just about everyone can use an occasional communications skills "tune-up," and if you wait until your relationship is in crisis, you'll face much harder work than if you'd been practicing your skills all along.

OWNING WHAT'S OURS

Nobody communicates with perfect form all of the time. But, when communication is loaded, difficult, confusing and important, then we need to make the ethical commitment to own our stuff, and let you own yours. That means we do not talk about, interpret, inventory, analyze, judge or otherwise trample all over your stuff. In formal communication we promise to stay with what is ours, our feelings, that we own, and give our partners the respect to let them represent their own feelings, their inner reality, their truth.

When you are willing to own your distress, it becomes possible for your partner to comfort you, to offer you reassurance and love when things are hard — so that even when you don't agree about how you are going to handle an issue, you can still exchange love and comfort. We recommend that everyone be open about asking for reassurance, love, hugs, comfort and stuff like that. Many of us grew up in families where we were taught not to ask for what we needed, scorned, perhaps, as only wanting attention.

So what's wrong with wanting attention? Isn't there plenty? Remember about starvation economies: don't short-change yourself. You do not have to be content with little dribs and drabs of comfort, attention, support, reassurance and love. You get to have all the comfort and reassurance you want. You and your intimates can set yourselves up to share lots and lots and lots, and in the process learn how much more you have to share than you ever thought. So focus on abundance, and create your environmental ecology rich in the good things of life — warmth and love and sex.

How to F*** up

We have the following guide of carefully tested methods for making mistakes in polyamorous relationships. With proper application and ingenuity, these methods may impair or destroy monogamous relationships as well; they're truly multipurpose tools. We post this listing for your consideration; no liability expressed or implied.

1. Lie. This is basic and effective. To maximize bad results, lie about something important to the other person(s) and arrange to be caught in the lie in such a way as to produce maximum shock. Additional stress points awarded for keeping the lie going for a while before discovery, which increases the disorientation and sense of betrayal in the deceived person(s). Lying about sex gets double points. Lying about being married gets triple f***-up points. Creative lies of omission (i.e. "not telling") with fancy rationalizations and condescension get gold stars.

2. Avoid self-knowledge. This is more elegant than strategy 1, as it combines a bold sweep of denial with sorties of distraction aimed at oneself. This tactic is most effective when combined with tactics 3 and 4. Self-destructive or addictive behaviour has also been found very effective in avoiding self-knowledge. When combined with an endearing attitude of helplessness, this strategy has been proven efficacious in attracting "rescuers" or "white

KNIGHTS" ON WHOM ONE CAN THEN PRACTICE STRATEGIES 4 AND 3, IN THAT ORDER.

3. BLAME THE OTHER PERSON(S). IF ANYTHING WENT WRONG, HEY, IT MUST BE THEIR FAULT, RIGHT? THIS ELIMINATES THE NEED FOR MESSY THINGS LIKE COMMUNICATION AND NEGOTIATION, WHICH CAN BE EMBARRASSING, PARTICULARLY IF ONE IS USING STRATEGY 2.

4. DISCLAIM RESPONSIBILITY. THIS IS A LITTLE MORE COMPLEX THAN STRATEGY 3, AND OFTEN INCLUDES WHAT IS REFERRED TO AS "CODEPENDENCY." THE CLASSIC WAY TO PLAY THIS STRATEGY IS TO CATER TO THE PARTNER(S) INVOLVED WHILE REPRESSING ONE'S OWN DESIRES AND QUESTIONS. THIS ALLOWS A GOOD HEAD OF RESENTMENT TO BUILD UP, AND ONE CAN JUSTIFY ANGER BY SAYING ONE HAS DONE SO *MUCH* FOR ONE'S PARTNER(S) AND GETS NO THANKS, ETC. IN ITS MOST REFINED STATE, THIS STRATEGY MAKES THE OTHER PERSON(S) RESPONSIBLE FOR SETTING THE DIRECTION, PACE AND CONTENT OF THE RELATIONSHIP, FOR WHICH ONE CAN THEM BLAME THEM IF ONE'S OWN EXPECTATIONS OR NEEDS ARE NOT MET. USING STRATEGY 2 TO AVOID KNOWLEDGE OF THESE EXPECTATIONS AND NEEDS GETS DOUBLE POINTS.

5. PUSH. THIS IS AN ART, ALBEIT A CRUDE ONE. WHEN AUGMENTED WITH STRATEGY 6, PUSHING CAN ACHIEVE SPECTACULAR NEGATIVE RESULTS IN EVEN A SHORT TIME. REMEMBER, WHEN PUSHING, ONLY *YOUR* SATISFACTION COUNTS! IT'S A DOG-EAT-DOG WORLD, AND YOU'RE A PIT BULL. EMOTIONAL AND MENTAL BULLYING CAN BE AS SATISFYING AS OLD-FASHIONED PHYSICAL COERCION, AND NOT NEARLY AS EASILY PROSECUTABLE. *(CONT'D)*

6. PLAY ON INSECURITY. THIS IS AN OLD FAVORITE. USING SEXUAL INSECURITY AS A WEAPON AND COMBINING THIS WITH STRATEGY 5 IS A FOUR-STAR WINNER. ATTEMPTING TO CONTROL ONE'S PARTNER(S) BY MANIPULATING THEM THROUGH THEIR INSECURITIES IS A SURE-FIRE F***-UP TACTIC. IT'S SO MUCH MORE DELICATE THAN SIMPLY BEATING THEM UP, TOO, THOUGH THE RESULTANT EMOTIONAL DAMAGE CAN BE REMARKABLY SIMILAR.

7. AVOID INTIMACY. THIS MAY SEEM PARADOXICAL; AFTER ALL, WE'RE TALKING ABOUT GETTING UP-CLOSE AND PERSONAL WITH AS MANY HOT BI BABES — ER, AHEM — WE'RE DISCUSSING ACHIEVING SATISFYINGLY CLOSE RELATIONSHIPS WITH A NUMBER OF PEOPLE, RIGHT? THE TRICK OF AVOIDING INTIMACY CAN BE PERFORMED IN SEVERAL WAYS, BUT THE EASIEST IS TO CONFUSE INTIMACY WITH "RUBBING SLIPPERY BITS TOGETHER." SUBSTITUTE THE WORDS "SEX" AND "LOVE" FOR EACH OTHER OFTEN IN CONVERSATIONS. REPEAT THE MANTRA, "IF YOU LOVED ME, YOU'D KNOW WHAT I WANT." PRACTICE STRATEGY 8 ASSIDUOUSLY, SUPPLEMENTING IT WITH STRATEGY 2. ACCORDING TO THE NEEDS OF THE MOMENT, FIGURE OUT WHETHER ACTION OR WORDS ARE MORE LIKELY TO BE AMBIGUOUS OR MISCONSTRUED, AND GO WITH WHAT GIVES YOU THE MOST PLAUSIBLE DENIABILITY LATER. SOME EXCEPTIONALLY TALENTED INDIVIDUALS MANAGE TO GIVE THE IMPRESSION OF BEING INTIMATE WHILE SUCCESSFULLY REMAINING STONE-COLD. STUDY SALES TECHNIQUES FOR POINTERS. PEOPLE WITH GOOD "LINES" FALL INTO THIS CATEGORY, ESPECIALLY IF THE LINES INCLUDE EXPLANATIONS OF HOW THEY TRULY *VALUE* THE OTHER PERSON.

8. DON'T TALK. TALKING HAS BEEN KNOWN TO LEAD TO COMMUNICATION IF PRACTICED CARELESSLY. **C**OMMUNICATION WILL SERIOUSLY IMPAIR YOUR F***-UP PROGRESS, AND IN CERTAIN CASES WILL HALT OR REVERSE IT ENTIRELY. **I**F YOU *MUST* TALK, USE CLICHES AND QUOTATIONS FROM POPULAR SONGS AS MUCH AS POSSIBLE, OR FALL BACK ON STRATEGY NUMBER **1**.

IF ALL ELSE FAILS, MAKE A SAFER-SEX AGREEMENT WITH YOUR PARTNER(S) AND THEN BREAK IT, CONTRACTING A COMMUNICABLE DISEASE ABOUT WHICH YOU DO NOT THEN TELL THEM. **D**OUBLE POINTS FOR AVOIDING ALL DISCUSSION OR NEGOTIATION OF SEXUAL MATTERS ENTIRELY SO THAT THE "AGREEMENT" IS WISHFUL THINKING AND COMPLETELY DENIABLE. **F**OR A COUP DE GRACE, ADD STRATEGY **6** AND TELL THEM IT WOULDN'T HAVE HAPPENED IF THEY HAD BEEN SATISFYING YOU LIKE THEY WERE SUPPOSED TO.

9. FOR THE ULTIMATE METAF***-UP, REMAIN TECHNICALLY FAITHFUL TO YOUR PARTNER WHILE BREAKING THE SPIRIT OF WHATEVER AGREEMENT YOU HAVE WHENEVER POSSIBLE, KEEPING THIS KNOWLEDGE BOTTLED UP TO ENSURE MAXIMUM FEAR, SHAME AND RESENTMENT. **S**OME PEOPLE WIN THE GRAND PRIZE WITH THE FIGLEAF-AND-STINGING-NETTLE CLUSTER FOR SELF-INFLICTED SUFFERING AND WASTED POTENTIAL BY MANAGING TO KEEP THIS STRATEGY UP UNTIL DEATH DO THEM PART, CONCEALING FROM THEIR SPOUSE THE FACT THAT THEY HAVE BEEN SHAMMING HAPPINESS ALL THESE YEARS.

— *COURTESY* **E***LISE* **M***ATTHESEN*

CHAPTER 6. AGREEMENTS

Most successful relationships, from casual acquaintanceship through lifetime monogamy, are based on assumptions that are really unstated agreements about behavior: you don't kiss your mailman, you don't tip your mother. These are the unspoken rules we learn very early in our lives, from our parents, our playmates and our cultures. People who break these unspoken rules are often considered odd, sometimes even crazy, because the values and judgments behind the social agreements about how we relate to one another are so deeply ingrained that we are usually not even aware that we have made any agreement at all.

In many day-to-day relationships, such as your relationship with neighbors and co-workers, it's probably fine to rely on those implicit, "built-in" agreements. But when you're trying something as complicated and unprecedented as ethical sluthood, we think it's very important to take nothing for granted. Talk with the people in your life about your agreements, and negotiate the conditions, environments and behaviors that will get your own needs met.

You'll often hear people talking about the "rules" of their relationships. But "rules" implies a certain rigidity, that there is a right way and a wrong way to run your relationship, and that there will be penalties if you do it wrong. We understand that there are many different ways that people may choose to relate to each other, so we prefer to use the word "agreements" to describe mutually agreed-upon, conscious decisions, designed to be flexible enough to accommodate individuality, growth and change. These agreements are sometimes a little fuzzy, particularly if you're used to the hard edges of rules. A little fuzziness is OK; your agreement will either get clarified later if it needs to be — or it won't, in which case it's probably clear enough.

How do you know when you need an agreement? You can tell by listening to your emotions. If something comes up that leaves you feeling icky or angry or unheard or whatever, that's an area in which you and your partner may need to discuss making an agreement. We suggest that you let go right now of the idea that you can predict every single situation that might come up in your relationship and make a rule to cover it — just forget it. Many perfectly good agreements get made by 20-20 hindsight: a problem comes up, and instead of arguing over whose fault it was, the couple simply makes an agreement to try to prevent that problem from coming up again.

Our friends Laurie and Chris have become extraordinarily flexible agreement-makers through practicing a lot:

> We met at the Renaissance Faire and made a pretty deep connection right away. Although we didn't feel ready to jump into marriage right off, we did get handfasted [an ancient Celtic rite of romantic commitment] about five months after we met. Our handfasting included an agreement that if we still wanted to be together a year and a day later, we'd get married. And we did.
>
> When we first decided to get handfasted, Chris proposed an agreement in which we'd be free to be

sexual with other people during Faire, but at no other time. Laurie felt shocked by his desire to do this, and insecure about what might happen. So we decided to postpone a decision until the next summer's Faire, after we'd gotten married. During the first year of our marriage, the agreement was for Faire only, and then after that we extended it to the weekend preparatory workshops as well as to Faire itself. At one of these, Laurie met a guy with whom she got fairly seriously involved — it was our first ongoing relationship outside the marriage. At that point things opened up all the way to where Laurie was spending a lot of her time with her other lover, and Chris didn't like it much; he felt that he wasn't getting enough time with Laurie.

So we renegotiated. We decided that either of us could sleep over with another partner twice a month. We felt that twice a month was often enough for fun, but not so often that it would accommodate a threateningly strong bond with someone else. That's been working pretty well for a while, although we've compromised on a case-by-case basis a time or two.

We're still working out the bugs — among other things, we're hoping to become parents pretty soon, and we're not sure how a baby will affect our relationship. But our agreements have always been at least tolerable, and at times they've offered a relief valve that's kept us from fleeing the relationship in terror!

CONSENT

So what constitutes a good agreement? In our opinion, the single most important hallmark of agreement is *consent*, which we define as "an active collaboration for the pleasure and well-being of all concerned." In the case of polyamory, this consent often includes that of people not directly involved — primary partners, children and other parties whose lives are affected by your agreements.

Defining consent can sometimes be tricky. If someone consents under pressure, we don't think that meets the "active collaboration" criterion. And you can't consent to something you don't know about: "Well, you didn't say I *couldn't* fly to Boise for two weeks with this flight attendant I just met" does not constitute consent.

In order to achieve this kind of active consent, it is critical that everyone involved accept responsibility for knowing their own feelings and communicating them. This isn't always easy. Sometimes feelings don't want to be pulled to the surface and examined — you may simply know that you feel bad. Give yourself the time and support you need to manifest that feeling, perhaps using some of the strategies we discussed in the "Jealousy" chapter. If you feel like you need help in defining what's going on for you, it's OK to ask for that help: physical or verbal reassurance often make a huge difference, and sometimes a wise friend or therapist can ask the right questions to help you untangle a complicated feeling. Once you start listening to your own feelings, you'll have a much easier time getting your needs and desires out there where everybody can hear them and make agreements to help meet them.

Most of us need some support in asking for what we want. When we are involved in making agreements, we need to feel safe that the needs we reveal will not be held against us. Most of us feel pretty vulnerable in and around our emotional limits, but it's important to recognize that these limits are valid, too: "I need to feel loved," "I need to feel that I'm important to you," "I need to know that you find me attractive," "I need you to listen and care about me when I feel hurt."

Blaming, manipulation, bullying and moral condemnation do not belong in the agreement-making process. The process of making a good agreement must include a commitment from all concerned to listen to one another's concerns and feelings in an open and unprejudiced way. If you are waiting for your partner to reveal a weakness so that you can exploit it into ammunition to "win" your argument, you are not ready to do a satisfactory agreement.

Legalistic hair-splitting is another enemy of good agreements. We know one couple whose agreement was that either of them would let the other one know within twenty-four hours if they were going to have sex with someone else. One of them called the other one from another city to let her know that he'd had sex with someone else the night before. "But you said you'd give me twenty-four hours' notice!" she cried angrily. "I never said twenty-four hours *before*," he pointed out. This "loophole-finding" legalistic behavior left neither individual feeling that their agreement had worked for them. The moral: be clear, be specific, and above all negotiate in good faith. This is not about cheating any more.

Agreements need to be realistic, something that you really can keep. It is unrealistic to ask your partner to never enter into a sexual interaction with a person that they care about "too much." There is no way to define "too much," and few of us conceive of our polyamorous utopia as a world in which you are only allowed to share sex with people you don't care about at all. None of us can truthfully agree to feel only this way or that way: our agreements need to have room in them for real emotions, whatever they may be.

Agreements do not have to be equal. People are different and unique, and what pushes my buttons might be perfectly okay with you. So one person might find it very important that his partner not stay out overnight, whereas said partner might actually enjoy an occasional opportunity to watch the late movie by himself and eat crackers in bed. One friend of ours says,

> Bill and I have very different needs when it comes to relationships. I feel no need to be monogamous; I'm quite comfortable having sex with people I like, but they're not affairs of the heart — whereas his sexual connections are either very casual, like at parties, or very deep and long-term. We've formed agreements that meet both of our needs — mine for friendly partners and fuck buddies, his for long-term secondary relationships.

So fairness does not mean equity. Fairness means we care about how each person feels, and make agreements to help all of us feel as good as possible.

When thinking about agreements for an open relationship, most people start out by listing what their partner can and cannot do: don't kiss her on the mouth, don't ever treat him better than you do me. Some "thou shalt nots" *are* necessary: agreements need to be made, for example, about sexual connections with relatives, neighbors and coworkers, and I really care a lot that you refrain from seducing my boss. And my therapist, too. But many negative agreements are really about protecting your partner from feeling hurt or jealous. The best agreements to protect your partner from emotional pain are positive:

let's have a special date next weekend, I will find time to listen to you when you hurt, I'll tell you how much I love you again and again.

Thinking up agreements that will help both partners feel emotionally safe can be confusing, since in the process of unlearning jealousy we will all at some time be asking our partners to agree to take some risk, to feel some painful feelings, to fall down a few times in order to learn how to ride the emotional bicycle of truly free love. And we all need a sense of emotional safety to succeed at feeling secure in open relationships.

One way you can make agreements to respect emotional limits is to ask for whatever seems like it might make you feel a *little bit* safer — reassurance, compliments, affection, a special ritual for homecoming after a date — and then when that works and you feel a little safer, take another step toward even more safety, and soon you will feel safe enough to expand your explorations further and further. Each tiny step in the direction of freedom will eventually get you there. One of the things that works about reassurance is that once we understand that our partner, or partners, or maybe even also their partners, are willing to help us with our feelings, we feel more secure and need less and less protection as we go along.

The single most important thing to remember about agreement-making is that the purpose of an agreement is to find a way in which everybody can win.

SOME AGREEMENTS

We've done some asking around among our friends and colleagues to find out what kinds of relationship agreements have worked for others. Here's a partial list of agreements we've heard from some very successful sluts. Notice as you read it how many different kinds of agreements it contains — some are sexual, some are relationship-oriented; some "thou shalts" and some "thou shalt nots"; some are logistical and some sentimental. Just so you know that we're not recommending any of these, you should also note that some are mutually exclusive. We're presenting this list as a discussion-opener, not as how it ought to be.

- everybody *has* to make some agreements about sexual health
- call nobody else by a particular pet name
- everybody will work together to find a good place for the non-involved partner to be
- no sleepovers (always spend night together except while traveling)
- I'll watch everyone's kids this weekend, you do it next weekend
- you don't get to use our car for dates with your other lover
- no intercourse with other partners
- no genital contact with other partners
- no anal contact with other partners
- no kissing with other partners
- veto power over potential other partners
- advance notice of potential other partners
- previous discussion required
- don't tell me about other partners
- tell me everything you did with other partners
- other partners must be same-sex/opposite-sex
- everybody meets everybody — no strangers
- group sex only
- anonymous sex only
- committed sex only

- must check in to confirm safety after get-together with new partner
- everybody chips in for the babysitter
- Friday nights only
- Saturday nights are for us
- be sure to save some hot sexual energy for me
- not in our bed
- no surprises
- lover will not contact other lover without mutual lover's knowledge
- if non-involved lover feels lonely or left out, he will ask to participate
- not in our house
- limits on phone calls, 'Net time, etc.
- establish quality time, time to fight, time to discuss, dates, etc.
- only at parties
- we'll set *our* next date before we have one with someone else
- agreements about who can talk about what to whom
- not during time we would otherwise be spending together
- don't take off the ring I gave you
- little gifts and cards help
- limits about partner choice — neighborhood? school? work? relatives? close friends? total strangers? partner's doctor, lawyer, therapist?
- only in my presence
- we'll spend an hour cuddling and reconnecting afterwards

Predictability

Our experience is that most people need some kind of predictability to deal with the stresses of open relationships. Most of us can handle a nervous-making situation much better if we know when it is going to happen, and when it is going to be over. We can plan to do something supportive with a friend, go to a movie, visit Mom, whatever — and tell ourselves that we only have to handle things for this chunk of time, and then our sweetie will come back and maybe we can plan a celebratory reunion.

Most people have a harder time dealing with surprises, which can feel like land mines exploding. Very few of us would be comfortable living with the possibility that our partner might go home with someone else at any time, from any party we go to, from the restaurant where we thought we were just going for a cup of coffee — no place, no time would be secure.

If you feel that planning takes too much of the spontaneity out of your life, then think about declaring one weekend a month to be open season, or one Saturday night, or whatever — then you can make a decision whether to join your partner in cruising or sit this one out in a quieter milieu. An agreement to be unpredictable at some specified time is, after all, predictable.

What if there is no agreement?

There are probably a lot of things in your life on which you feel no need to reach agreement. Most people don't feel the need to agree on whether to wear red or blue, or whether to eat crunchy or smooth peanut butter. However, lack of agreement can feel less comfortable in the close-to-the-bone field of sexual relationships.

Still, sometimes, you simply need to agree *not* to agree. Between the "yes" of full agreement and the "no" of full disagreement is a whole big gray area of no-agreement-yet, or tolerable-disagreement, or even who-cares? Sometimes you will eventually find it possible to make an agreement, and other times you won't. But you've been getting along fine without agreement so far, and there's a pretty good chance you can go on that way almost indefinitely.

Occasionally, however, you might hit an area in which agreement is both necessary and impossible. For many people, the whole issue of non-monogamy may be one of these; childbearing is another frequent "deal-breaker." We suggest compromise-seeking (possibly with the help of a qualified therapist) and flexibility. But if agreement simply cannot be reached, we think the skills you learned in trying to reach agreement — the non-blaming, non-judging and non-manipulating — can also stand you in very good stead as you agree to change or even end whatever relationship you're in. Sometimes, when you agree to end *that* relationship, you may find that you can agree on a new kind of relationship — some of our best friends (and hottest lovers) are our exes.

GETTING TO "YES"

(Yes, we stole this phrase from somebody else.) So how do you find an agreement that will work for everybody? A good place to start is by defining your goals. A goal is not the same as an agreement; your goal is what you're trying to accomplish, your agreement is the means you're using to try to get there. So, for example, if your goal is to prevent anyone from feeling taken advantage of, your agreements might have to do with ensuring that nobody's personal time, space or belongings are being infringed on.

Often, you discover a goal by tripping over a problem: "Last night, when you and Sam were in our bedroom together, my feet were freezing and I couldn't get in there to get my bedroom slippers." The goal is to prevent this problem from coming up again — what kinds of agreements might help achieve that goal? Answering these questions will require an honest (and often difficult) look at what the *real* problem is: is it that your feet are cold, or that you resent being kicked out of your own bedroom, or that you're feeling jealous and left out?

Once you've defined your problem and your goal, it's time to start figuring out a good agreement. It might be appropriate to do a "trial" agreement — to put a time limitation on your newborn agreement to see how it feels to everybody concerned. After the time is up, whether that's a week or a year, you can sit down again to discuss what worked, what didn't, and whether to continue your agreement or revise it or scrap it.

In our experience, it's rare for an agreement to last a lifetime without change: human beings change, and so do agreements. The way you can tell that your agreement needs to change is when someone doesn't agree to it any more. Catherine and her partner, for example, began their relationship with an agreement that they could be sexual with other people, but that they couldn't fall in love with anyone else. Then one of them did. (In hindsight, this seems like a fairly silly agreement — as though you could simply decide not to fall in love!) She remembers,

> There was a period in which we were having "check-ins" one or two times a day. This was a situation neither of us had ever planned on. We found it was very important to stay in the moment, and to stay with tangible

things — yes, it feels OK if she sleeps over while I'm out of town; no, it doesn't feel right for you to bring the two of us to the same party. We found, during that experience as well as a similar one more recently, that the words "in love with" were kind of a trap, and made us both feel kind of panicky — that agreements that dwell on measurable factors such as time, behavior and space work better for us.

Expect to spend some time working out your agreements. Expect to hear things from your lover(s) that you didn't expect; expect to hear things from yourself that are also surprising. A gay couple we know started negotiating for opening their relationship, and discovered a big difference in their expectations of how that openness would work. One man's image of nonmonogamy was that outside involvements would be limited to one-night stands with strangers, while the other man envisioned a friendly circle of fuck buddies. This couple is currently enjoying monogamy while they discuss their way onto some more common ground.

Expect to try out some agreements and find out that they don't work, and expect to need to change them. You will get better at this process with practice, and in time you will know your own and your partners' needs so well that negotiating agreements will be easy. But in the beginning, while you are learning, tidiness won't count anywhere near as much as tolerance.

When you first set out, some of these discussions may get quite heated: remember, anger is an emotion that tells you what is important to you. What is constructive about these difficult times is what you learn about your partners and about yourself. Don't get discouraged — all the successful sluts you see who seem so carefree have fought over their agreements. You too can work your way through this tangled web of assumptions and emotions, and learn to love with openness and freedom.

PART III – SLUTS IN THE WORLD

CHAPTER 1. A SLUT'S-EYE VIEW

From the slut's point of view, the world is sometimes a dangerous place. Lots of people seem to think it is okay to go to any lengths to stop us from being sexual. Some anti-sex crusaders try to make loving dangerous for women by outlawing birth control and abortion, leading to unwanted pregnancies and back-alley medical care. Others would outlaw access to sex information, in schools or on the Internet, so that our children cannot learn to care for their health and well-being, and have no access to safer sex training that would teach them how to avoid spreading AIDS. Some people purporting to have the word from God preach on the public airwaves that AIDS is a just punishment for any sexuality that deviates from what these self-proclaimed godly folk believe is normal. We find this truly obscene.

There are places where some people believe that being a slut makes you fair game for violence. Why were you walking down that street at night in a short dress, or tight pants? No wonder you got raped, or assaulted. Must be the victim's fault. And you look so queer — no wonder that gang decided to beat you up.

We are also considered fair game for other forms of oppression. Multiple sexual partners can be seen as a good excuse to take all of your property, your children and your future income in a punitive divorce settlement. And don't forget to keep your social life a secret on the job.

You could lose your job, or your promise for advancement, or your professional reputation, if you share your personal life with the wrong person.

JUDGING OURSELVES

We hope this examination of the dangers of sluttery will lead you to ask yourself some questions. What is my experience of oppression and how does it affect me? Who do I have to lie to in my life? How does this affect me? What are my closets? And as you look deeper, you might ask yourself: what assumptions have I made about how my sexuality should be? Do I have judgments about what "good" and "nice" people do that I wind up turning against myself?

When we judge ourselves by cultural values imposed from the outside, when women believe they ought to be small and quiet, when gay people believe that their sexual choice is a neurosis, or when we all believe we would be better people if we were able to be monogamous, this is internalized oppression. When we apply these unfair judgments to other people who are like us, when we see our friends as *too* slutty or *too* free, this is called horizontal hostility. We suggest you look through the preceding section on myths, stereotypes and oppression as a checklist, to see where your own beliefs that you learned in our sex-negative culture might be getting in your way.

SANCTIONS AGAINST SLUTS

Those of us who choose to run our lives and loves in an unconventional manner should probably be prepared for the fact that many parts of the world will not welcome us with open arms. While there are certainly ways to protect yourself against some social, logistical and financial consequences, we can't guarantee that there never will be consequences. It's not easy being easy.

Ex-spouses, parents, in-laws, and others who don't share your values about the potential for inclusive relationships may be hostile. Your friendly neighborhood pastor may not be sympathetic, either. And bringing both of your partners to the company picnic is not a good way to ensure your continued ascent through the corporate hierarchy. We recommend extreme caution in choosing who to come out to: yes, we know you're blissfully happy and want to share your joy with the world, but remember, you can't un-tell. We know people who have lost jobs, child custody and more because the wrong people have become aware of their sexual choices.

Some landlords are quite reluctant to rent to groups that don't conform to the traditional family structure; although this may be technically illegal, in our experience it's common, and we suggest that you be prepared to tell a teeny white lie when necessary. ("Why, yes, he's my adopted brother. Oh, that? Well, I use my married name...") Some leases contain clauses that allow landlords to terminate rental agreements on the basis of "immoral behavior" or "association with undesirable people," and most allow them to kick you out for illegal behavior — which in some states includes non-marital sex and/or sodomy.

Similarly, your personal love and sex arrangements are best kept out of the workplace: both of us have lost jobs and clients for being who we are. While some cities and states offer some protection to people who are gay, lesbian or transgender, we are not aware of any that guarantee equal rights for sluts. Unless you are absolutely certain that your employer or your co-worker is slut-positive — not just that she's a swell person with a great fund of dirty jokes, or that he used to sleep around in college — we recommend a capacious and well-insulated closet.

GOVERNMENT IS NOT OUR FRIEND

As we write this, our nation's various political establishments are wrestling over the issue of whether people of the same gender ought to be able to partake in the financial and social benefits of legal marriage. (With any luck, we'll be able to edit that statement out of future editions of this book.)

While we certainly think that same-sex couples are entitled to the same benefits as opposite-sex couples, we strongly question what business any of this is of the government's. For several centuries, government has subtly or not-so-subtly attempted to enforce its ideas of what constitutes a proper relationship between human beings, by offering a financially and socially desirable legal status only to those who meet its criteria. As a result, we've seen laws that forbid marriage between people of different races, laws that give preferred tax status to married couples (Dossie remembers tax laws that gave widows lower taxes than single parents), laws that dictate exactly how married couples must share their money and belongings, laws that tell you what gender of person you're allowed to marry, laws that tell you what *number* of persons you're allowed to marry, and many other coercive laws – even laws that tell you you're married when you didn't choose to be, like common-law marriage. In order to be allowed to be a state at all, the territory of Utah had to pass laws that only two people were allowed in a marriage, nullifying an honored tradition of Mormon polygamy. (Some Mormon groups, we hear, still live in established multi-partner marriages in defiance of those laws. Good for them!)

We see marriage laws imposed by the government as a blatant violation of the Constitutional separation of church and state, as well as a very bad environment for sluttery. We think that most people are able to figure out and codify their own contractual agreements — agreements that specify how they will share their belongings, make their decisions, raise their children, care for their sick and elderly, and arrange for their futures together. And, for those who can't or don't want to do the work of figuring all that out from scratch, we know there are churches, support groups, mediators, publications and other resources to help create agreements that meet their standards.

OK, end of rant. You know and we know that our government is not likely to get out of the marriage business anytime soon. In the meantime, however, those of us who are too slutty, too queer or too cynical to buy into this one-male one-female till-death-do-us-part model had best learn to make our own agreements, and to deal with the real-world ramifications of doing without official "support" for our chosen lifestyles.

LEGAL AGREEMENTS

If you and your partner(s) are living in a somewhat marriage-like structure, with the expectation of sharing property, providing for one another in the event of illness or death, raising children, or running a business together, we strongly recommend official legal documentation of your status and intentions. Terrifying stories of lover kept from lover when someone gets hospitalized, a longtime partner left penniless and homeless after someone's unexpected death, individuals who have been parents in all ways but blood losing an orphaned child to a partner's parents or ex-spouse, and so on, should be enough to convince you that it's time to get official about all this.

You do not legally own your children, and the legal agreements you can make about them are limited by that fact. You can use your will to express your desires about who will care for your children after your death, but the court may not be obliged to follow your wishes. In some cases a non-biological parent can adopt a lover's children as a step-parent. But your children are not property, and you cannot give them to anyone you choose.

Aside from that, it is possible, and not difficult, to make fully legal contracts to document your agreements on relationship issues. A publishing company called Nolo Press specializes in do-it-yourself legal books, complete with forms and step-by-step instructions. Catherine and her partner have chosen not to engage in legal marriage although, since they're an opposite-sex couple, they could do so; instead, they used the "Legal Guide for Lesbian and Gay Couples" (listed in the Bibliography) to outline their legal agreements with powers of attorney and wills.

Pay special attention to durable powers of attorney for finance and health care, and to wills. While the law will not support everything an eager slut might want to do with his money and property, your chances of having your desires upheld by the law will be greatly improved if you express them in a formal legal manner.

If your agreements are particularly complicated, or if things of great value (such as a lot of money or a successful business) are involved, you may want to go beyond the do-it-yourself level and contact an attorney. If you have that kind of money, you probably know more about this than we do. Do try to find an attorney who is open to non-traditional relationships.

We have neither the space nor the expertise to tell you all the ways that people with non-traditional sexualities can go about setting up their lives — options range all the way from adopting your partner to setting up a business trust, and beyond. But please, don't assume that your good intentions, heartfelt love and general wonderfulness will protect you. Sluts don't have that luxury. Do your homework and get the law on your side.

CHAPTER 2. HEALTH

In this dangerous era, the term "safe sex" has taken on a specific meaning — "sex designed to minimize the risk of HIV transmission." But sex has *never* been altogether safe. Both your authors are old enough to have grown up in an era when an unwanted pregnancy meant a life-endangering illegal abortion. It's been only a few decades since more reliable birth control became available, and only a few before that since antibiotics began curing illness, insanity and death caused by sexually transmitted diseases (STDs). Seen in historical perspective, today's environment, in which careless sex can kill, is the norm, not the exception. Which means that you have to protect yourself and your partners.

Given that sex is never completely safe, ethical sluts put time, effort and commitment into getting as much sex at as little risk as possible. Hence, the term "safer sex" has sprung into use, and is the term we have used throughout this book to refer to the many risk-reduction strategies that can help minimize the chances of infection and/or unwanted pregnancy.

Some of the safer-sex information out there these days refers to AIDS as though that were the only infection you had to worry about. It isn't. Thus, we're not going to spend a lot of time debating which forms of sexual expression are likelier than others to transmit HIV — first, the information available on this topic changes almost weekly and would undoubtedly be obsolete by the time this book sees print; and second, you need to protect yourself against HIV *and* against herpes, hepatitis, gonorrhea, syphilis, chlamydia, shigella, human papilloma virus, cervical cancer, unwanted pregnancy and a host of other nasties.

On the other hand, we don't think it's necessarily a good idea to tell you to cover every portion of your anatomy with latex before you touch another human being. Such advice smacks a bit to us of "Just say no," and we think people often react to such blithe blanket advice with an all-or-nothing shrug — they're not willing to follow it to the letter, so they don't follow it at all and wind up sick or dead.

Still, there *are* ways to continue to have hot satisfying sex without performing the erotic equivalent of skydiving with a faulty parachute. Here are some that we, and the people we know, have used successfully.

FLUID BONDING

A strategy used by some sluts who are in a primary relationship is called "fluid bonding" or "fluid monogamy." Both of us have such agreements with our life partners. To do this kind of agreement, both (or all) partners get thoroughly tested for HIV and other diseases. This may mean waiting six months to be sure, since HIV antibodies don't reliably show up in the bloodstream for that long after the individual is infected. Once you're both sure you're healthy, you agree to practice unprotected sex with one another, but to use barriers (condoms, gloves, dental dams and so on) with others. Be sure you're in clear agreement about which activities are safe enough to do without a barrier and which ones require a barrier; to reach such an agreement, everyone involved will have to do some homework on the risk levels of various activities, and decide together what level of risk is acceptable to you.

In addition, you may wish to restrict some kinds of sex – many people focus on vaginal and/or anal intercourse, which place the participants at higher risk for disease transmission – to your primary relationship.

Another good reason for fluid bonding is babymaking: if you and your primary partner are trying to become parents, you might not want to engage in potentially reproductive activities with all and sundry.

If barriers were infallible, fluid bonding would be a nearly perfect strategy. Unfortunately, they are not. Pinhole leaks can allow virus to creep through, although this happens less often than anti-sex crusaders would have you believe. Condoms can break or come off during sex. If you are fluid-bonded and experience a condom failure, you and your partner will have to decide together whether to begin again with HIV testing and six months of barrier usage, or to risk the possibility that one of you has been infected and could infect the other.

ELIMINATING HIGH-RISK BEHAVIORS

Another risk reduction strategy is simply to eliminate some forms of sexual expression from your repertoire. Many people have chosen to forego forms of sex that involve putting hands, mouths or penises into or near assholes, feeling that the particularly high risks of this form of play are not worth its rewards. (We note that medical journals have yet to include a case study of a dildo or butt plug coming down with a disease.) Others have decided not to engage in any form of penetration with an organic penis.

Every such decision you make requires that you balance your own desires against your assessment of the risks. Remember when you're making your decisions that desire is powerful and important, and that there's no point in making rules you can't live with – starving and binging is an even worse pattern for sluts than it is for dieters. On the positive side, expanding your range of hot sexual expression by learning new and exciting ways to have sex can leave you both safe and satisfied.

BARRIER USAGE

Many people decide to follow their sexual urges, but to be scrupulous about the use of latex or polyurethane barriers and other safer sex strategies. We hope you don't need us to explain this to you at this point in history, but careful use of barriers includes condoms for vaginal sex, anal sex and fellatio; gloves for masturbation of a male or female partner or for insertion of fingers into vaginas or anuses; and dental dams or plastic wrap for cunnilingus or analingus. It also includes placing a latex barrier (a glove or condom) over any sex toy that will be used by more than one person, and cleaning that toy thoroughly with an antiviral solution after each use.

The use of a good water-based lubricant can do wonders to make latexed sex more pleasurable for both or all partners. For tips on how to use barriers in a pleasure-enhancing manner, check out our chapter on sex and some of the books in the Bibliography. And if you're not completely comfortable using any of these barriers, practice! Gentlemen can masturbate with a condom (or two, or three), until it comes easy. We have heard of one dedicated fellow who managed to put on eighteen condoms at once — he said it felt really good. And why not get a little playful with your rubber?

After doing careful research into available information about the relative risks of various sexual behaviors, some people decide that some of these activities are safe enough to perform without a barrier. Safer sex workshops are available in most communities now, and the place where you get your HIV test will know where to find them. We urge thoughtfulness and conservatism in making such choices — we need all the readers we can get, so we don't want to lose you.

FINGER-CROSSING

Simply hoping for the best, or denying that you're at risk, or pretending that diseases and unwanted pregnancies only happen to other people, is *not* an acceptable strategy. If you don't have the honesty and courage to face the genuine risks of your sexual behaviors, you certainly don't have what it takes to be an ethical slut, and we question whether you should be having sex at all.

We are shocked and worried by the levels of denial we see among some sexual communities, who would like to believe that because HIV hasn't yet decimated them as it has the gay male community, they must be somehow immune. New strains of HIV are constantly being discovered, and it appears that transmission patterns may vary from one strain to the next — and even if you're not at particularly high risk for current strains of HIV, you certainly are for herpes, hepatitis and a host of other diseases. Get educated, friend, and take care of yourself.

TESTING AND PREVENTION

We think it's essential for ethical sluts to get tested for HIV and other sexually transmitted diseases on a regular schedule. How frequently depends on a number of risk factors in your life. Ask your doctor, clinic or Planned Parenthood office, and follow their advice.

While most STDs are preventable only with barriers and care, recent medical developments have evolved vaccinations that protect you against several potentially deadly forms of hepatitis. If you engage in non-monogamous anal play, these are a *very* good idea. They are expensive, but cheaper than getting sick. Get 'em.

BIRTH CONTROL

Mother Nature is called that for a reason — sometimes it seems like she wants everybody to be a parent. ("So, when are you going to give me a grandchild?")

Birth control technology is, alas, far from perfect: reliable, reversible, easy, side-effect-free contraception is still a dream. Unwanted pregnancies need no longer be the life-shattering tragedies of yesteryear, but they are still awful, and we hope that none of you ever has to have one.

If you are female, and have intercourse with men, and are not *certain* that you are not fertile, you must take active steps to ensure that you won't get pregnant until and unless you want to. Birth-control pills, longer-term chemical birth control like Norplant and Depo-Provera, diaphragms and cervical caps, condoms, IUDs, sponges and foam, tubal ligation, and other possibilities exist. Some women with regular menstrual cycles succeed at the rhythm method, particularly if they learn to enjoy outercourse during their fertile periods. There is a lot of good information available about the risks and reliability of all these methods; your physician, clinic, or Planned Parenthood can help you make a good choice.

For men who have intercourse with women, the choices are (unfortunately) quite limited. If you know you are unlikely to want to father children in the future, a vasectomy is minor surgery that will relieve you of a great deal of worry. If you hope to be a father someday, use those condoms — and lobby for research into better male contraception.

So what if someone gets pregnant anyway? This can be, to put it mildly, difficult. If the partners agree that an abortion is the best choice, that's pretty traumatic in and of itself; if there is disagreement, it can be shattering. Until such time as science enables men to carry fetuses in their bodies, we believe that the final decision has to be the woman's, but we bitterly sympathize with the man who would like to raise a baby and whose female partner isn't willing or able to carry it to term. We do think that both partners should share in the financial and emotional burden of an abortion or a pregnancy.

If one or both partners is interested in being a parent, and the woman is willing to carry the fetus to term, ethical sluthood opens up a wealth of options for parenting. Please don't feel that the only way to be a parent is to get married and buy a house in the suburbs — perfectly marvelous children come out of shared parenting arrangements, intentional communities, group marriages and a multitude of other ways to nurture and support a child. (More about this next chapter.)

COMMITTING TO HEALTHY SEX

You may notice that we have gone out of our way *not* to tell you what decisions to make about your sexual behavior. That's because only you can decide what risks feel acceptable to you, and we believe that letting anybody else make that decision for you virtually guarantees that you won't follow through on your choices.

You must, however, *make* choices. You must choose to do your homework, and learn what you need to know about risks and rewards. You must choose to do the work of saying "no" to sex that doesn't meet your own safety criteria, and of being prepared to say "yes" to sex that does: discovering you're out of condoms at the wrong moment is a recipe for disaster. You must choose to approach your sexual behaviors in a mature, realistic and *sober* manner — intoxication plays a major role in a shockingly high percentage of HIV infection and unwanted pregnancy.

And you must be prepared to share your sexual decision-making and history with any potential partners you encounter. If consent is at the core of ethical sluthood — and it is — your partners must be able to give informed consent to whatever risks are involved in having sex with you. You, of course, have the right to expect that same honesty from them.

You won't like talking about this stuff, especially not with a new lover. It's depressing and scary, definitely not erotic, and sometimes horrendously embarrassing. Allow us to reassure you: the first time is the worst. Practice makes perfect, and after you've been over all these ugly and lethal possibilities a few times, you will become less sensitive and learn to deal with what you need to with ease and grace. And it's well worth the investment: getting good at talking about sex has other rewards, like getting exactly what you want in the way of pleasure.

We, and most of the people we know, make fairly conservative choices about what health risks we take in our sexuality — and we know from experience that it is quite possible to have exciting, satisfying, fabulously slutty sex without lying awake nights worrying afterwards. And isn't that the kind of sex we all want to have?

CHAPTER 3. CHILDREARING

If you're raising kids today, you have it a little bit easier than sluts of yesteryear — images of families in books and television aren't quite as limited to "The Bobbsey Twins" and "Ozzie and Harriet" as they were in our childhoods. Still, even though divorce and single parents are now acceptable topics, our culture is being rather slow to catch up to the other realities of our lives: media images of multipartner relationships, same-sex relationships and other nontraditional models are still pretty rare.

Yet kids take to these relationships quite readily — perhaps more so than to the traditional nuclear family: children's need for tribe may be even more pronounced than adults'. Catherine remembers having some of her first desires for group living during vacations with her then-husband's extended family, when she noticed that her kids, surrounded by loving adults with plenty of time on their hands, were happier, more docile and less fragmented than she'd ever seen them. Today, she lives in a group household, and though her sons are nearly grown, they have adapted quite readily to the comings and goings of a disparate group of adults — one of whom is almost always free to answer a question, trouble-shoot a computer program, experiment with a recipe, or play a game.

In contrast to the dilemma of the traditional single parent who must decide how and if to bring sex partners back to the home she shares with her kids, the ethical slut may have a number of creative options for maintaining a fulfilling sex life while being a responsible parent. When Dossie was sharing a house with two other single mothers, one of her lovers used to babysit all the kids so the mothers had a chance to go out together. And one friend of ours used to babysit for her younger sister and the kids next door so that her parents could mess around with the next-door neighbors.

Still, many parents have a great deal of difficulty bridging the gap between responsible parenting and inclusive relationships. Questions about what and how much to tell your kids, how to prepare them for difficult questions in the outside world, and how to help them relate to the new people who arrive and depart in their lives can be challenging for any mom or dad.

We think that the most important characteristic you can bring to bear in the lives of your children is *consistency*. Kids, especially younger ones, don't deal well with here-today-gone-tomorrow connections. While it's easy to assume that inclusive relationships might create massive inconsistency, our experience is just the opposite. The binary nature of monogamy-centrist thinking tends, we think, to cause problems: you're either the love of my life, or you're out of here. Both of us have found that opening our lives to other kinds of connections also opens our children's lives. For example, a former lover of Catherine's has not been sexually involved with her for quite a while, but has become a sort of surrogate uncle and best friend to one of her sons and is still a loved member of her household — as she writes this, he is asleep on a futon on her living room floor.

SEX EDUCATION FOR KIDS

As you've surmised, we think inclusive emotional relationships can be highly beneficial to family life, and that children gain in role models, attention and support in the polyamorous extended family. Clearly, children should not be included in adult sexual behavior, and there are many adults around who have been wounded by sexual abuse as children who can testify to the damages. Children do, however, need enough information to make sense out of what the adults are doing, so they can grow up to their own healthy understanding of sexuality.

All parents must make their own decisions about what kind of sexual information their children should have at any given age. For the health and well-being of the child, a balance must be struck between offering too much information, which might seem scary or overwhelming, and too little, which might leave the child with the message that naked bodies and sexual arousal are so dangerous and embarrassing that it's not allowed to even talk about them. We don't want to terrify the kids, and we don't want them to come into their own adult sexual lives with the belief that sex is dirty and shameful.

To make matters more complicated, our culture currently is deeply divided about the entire subject of kids and sex. Some people consider any form of sex education to be child abuse, and many do not feel that children should have any information at all about adult sexual activities. Some authorities feel that when children have "precocious" information about sex, that must mean that the child is being abused by an adult. How are we to teach our children to say "no" to an abusive adult if we are not frank about what it is that they should say no to?

WHAT SHOULD THEY KNOW?

You'll have to decide how much your kids should know about your sexual choices, such as multiple partners, same-sex partners or alternative family structures. Our experience is that kids figure such things out quicker than you think they do, but that they may not figure them out exactly right. It's a delicate balance between giving your children enough information to answer their questions and allay their discomfort, and giving them too much information and thus frightening them or turning them off.

One word of warning: if your kids aren't old enough to keep such information to themselves, it may be best not to share it with them. One friend of ours, who had a lovely piercing placed in her clitoral hood as a symbol of commitment to her partner, was dismayed to find out that her very young daughter had told her schoolfriends and teachers that "Mommy has an earring in her penis." Fortunately, here in liberal San Francisco, no trouble ensued — but the ending might not have been so happy elsewhere. There are many places in this country where living in a nontraditional sexual lifestyle is considered a justification for legally removing your children from your custody. Even when you are sure you are doing no harm, you still may need to protect your kids from Mrs. Grundy.

WHAT SHOULD THEY SEE?

We think it's a good idea to model physical and verbal affection for children; that's how they learn to be affectionate adults. But you'll have to make some decisions about the appropriate dividing line between physical affection and sexual demonstrativeness.

Do your kids get to see you hugging your partners? Kissing them? Touching them? These are all decisions we can't make for you. You have to think them through yourself — taking into account such issues as their ages, their levels of sophistication, and their perceptions about your existing relationships — and abide by your own decisions.

Nudity is a gray area. We certainly don't think kids are seriously harmed by growing up in households where casual nudity is the norm. But a child who has never been around nude adults may be upset if nudity is suddenly introduced into his living arrangements. Kids are also very sensitive to issues like sexual display: if you sense that anybody is "strutting their stuff" instead of simply being comfortably nude, that's not a good environment for kids. Certainly, if a child expresses discomfort with being around your or your friends' nudity, her desires should be respected. And we hope it goes without saying that no child should ever be required to be nude in front of others — many children go through phases of extreme modesty as they struggle to cope with their changing bodies, and that, too, deserves scrupulous respect.

WHAT SHOULD THEY DO?

It is definitely inappropriate to allow your kids to engage in any form of sexual behavior with any of your partners, or vice versa. Many children go through one or more sexually explorative and/or flirtatious periods in their lives — this is natural and common. But it's very important that you and your friends maintain especially good boundaries during such periods; learning polite and friendly ways of acknowledging a child's changing needs without engaging sexually is a critical skill for any ethical slut who spends time around her own or her partners' kids. ("Isn't that cute? You're getting to be such a big girl now!")

ANSWERING THEIR QUESTIONS

Kids' questions about sex and relationships can often be challenging — from the five-year-old's "But how does the seed get *to* the egg?" to the teenager's "So how come you get to fuck anyone you want but I have to be home by midnight?"

Here's where the skills you've learned in other parts of this book can come in handy. You owe your kids honest, heartfelt responses to questions like these; this is not the time to come on all high-handed and parental. Particularly with older children and teenagers, it's fine to let them know if you're feeling ambivalent or embarrassed about something (they'll know anyway, believe us). If a situation makes you angry or sad, share that, too. They may need some reassurance that your emotion isn't their fault, and some reinforcement that it's not their job to help you feel better.

It's also fine to test their willingness to receive information. Before you start heaping data on their heads, you can try prefacing your communication with a question like, "Do you want to know about [whatever the topic is]?" Catherine remembers a conversation with her older son when he was about ten: she'd just done a "birds and bees" rap, and had perhaps gotten a little carried away. At the end of her long speech, she asked him, "So, as long as we're on this topic, is there anything else you want to know?" He replied, fervently, "Mom, you've already told me *much* more than I wanted to know."

Good boundaries are important here too. While your kids are certainly entitled to express an opinion about the way you choose to run your life, they don't get to dictate it. The flip side of this is that you owe it to them to help prevent their lives from being unduly impacted by a lifestyle they never chose. Dossie willingly agreed to maintain a discreet closet about her lesbian partner when her daughter's junior high school friends came to visit; her daughter got to "come out" to her friends about her mom at her own pace. Well, nobody ever said parenthood — especially slutty parenthood — was going to be easy.

PART IV – HAVING FUN

CHAPTER 1. FINDING PARTNERS

Just to prove to you that it *can* be done, we want to start this chapter with a true story of how a lesbian couple of our acquaintance began their relationship. They have lived together for two years now in a committed and polyamorous life partnership, and got married last August in a redwood grove. They are still very much in love, and have every intention of growing old together.

June had never been to a play party before. That's evidently what they call orgies in California, she mused. Well, at least it's a lesbian orgy. How on earth, she wondered, did I come to be the guest of honor at an orgy?

Actually, she knew how it came about. She was visiting her dear friend Flash in San Francisco, and Flash announced that she had the use of a house in the country for the weekend, and she wanted to throw a party and introduce June to her friends. Sounds like fun, thought June.... and then Flash began to talk about having a "Chick Rite" to celebrate the advent of spring by setting up mattresses and safer-sex supplies in the middle of the living room.

June had argued, and at first had refused to come. But Flash talked her into it, pointing out that she didn't have to actually have sex with anybody if she didn't want to. June finally said okay, adding that if she couldn't stand it she would hike down to the local coffeehouse with a book. So Flash went on setting up the house for the convenience of sexual pleasures, and June hid in the kitchen making dips, one party function that she at least understood.

As the guests began to arrive, June began to question whether or not she'd be able to stay at this event. She was introduced to a parade of the most outrageous dykes she had ever seen, femmes and butches like birds in bright plumage, sporting exotic garments designed to display a gallery of tattoos, gleaming here and there with jewelry set in body parts that June did not want to think about. And they were all so young! June felt the full weight of her forty-eight years. She figured you can't go wrong being polite, so she said the same how-do-you-dos she would anywhere else, wondering how she'd respond if one of these enthusiastic orgiasts actually told her how she did do.

In, at last, came a couple of women of unabashed middle age. One of them, Carol, was a dead ringer for June's Great-Aunt Mary — only Great-Aunt Mary would never have been seen in high butch gear complete with boots and cowboy hat. June felt relieved to have found one woman she could relate to. Then Carol smiled her most winning smile and announced that she would like to put her hand in June's cunt.

June, swallowing a gasp but ever polite, responded that she didn't really feel quite ready for that, and Carol, ever easygoing, replied "Okay, I'll check in with you later." Great Goddess, thought June, there's no escape. June knew about fisting, had learned to do it with a lover who liked it, she knew it was safe when done properly, but it seemed more than a little too intimate to try with someone whose name she'd only learned in the last half hour.

Then Lottie came in — close to June's age, but not dressed like it. Lottie sported a head of obviously dyed flaming red curls and a black chiffon dress through which could be clearly seen long black stockings, a black leather corset, and a voluptuosity of just plain flesh. How does she balance on those heels, wondered June, as Lottie hugged, kissed and chatted her way through the progressively less clothed mass of partygoers. June overheard Lottie thanking various women for their participation in a previous orgy held in celebration of Lottie's fiftieth birthday. Do these people ever get together and not have sex? wondered June.

Puppy piles began to form on the floor in front of the couch where June was sitting — untidy heaps of women necking and petting, smiling and laughing — Lottie and Carol conspicuously among them. June decided it would be safer out on the deck, where she might be able to soak out her terrors in the hot tub.

The hot tub was quieter, and June managed to chat with a few women, and began feeling marginally more comfortable. Then Lottie reappeared. Off came the dress, the stockings, the shoes — June found herself wondering what it would be like if she could see Lottie's cunt, and instantly wondered if anyone else had noticed her looking. Lottie slipped into the warm water, and almost immediately asked June if she would rub her neck, because it felt stiff. "Sure," she heard herself say, "I'd be happy to." Oh, no, she thought, what have I let myself in for?

Lottie's skin felt warm and silky under her fingers, and June rubbed and soothed. June felt relaxed by the rhythm of massage, and reassured as Lottie conversed about perfectly normal things: her work and June's, their philosophies of life: June's Buddhist, Lottie's pagan. Eventually, Lottie's neck relaxed, and the hot tub began to feel too warm, and Lottie brightly suggested they find out what was going on inside. She climbed out of the tub, pulled on her stockings and buckled her heels, and darted inside. Holy Minerva, thought June, can I follow her in there? No, she decided firmly, I can't. June found a table in a corner on the patio, and determinedly admired the stars.

Lottie, meanwhile, was finding she had a thing or two to think about as well. In the living room, her friends were happily disporting themselves on couches, in armchairs and in front of the fire, but Lottie was thinking about June. What is it about her that turns me on so much? Does she like me? Will she play with me? Doesn't look *like she's used to playing at parties — ah, well, there's always a first time. Now where did that girl go?*

Lottie scanned the living room, but there was no June to be found. The living room was actually pretty interesting, and Lottie contemplated giving up the chase and finding a friend to play with, but intrigue triumphed. She made her way toward the kitchen, stepping over various happy people and lingering here and there to appreciate some particularly exciting activity. Pausing to check out the dips and replenish her blood sugar, Lottie looked out the window and there was June, hiding out on the patio.

Ah, here's the opportunity, thought Lottie as she arranged a few goodies on a plate and trotted outside to share them with June. But, although they were chatting together quite amiably, Lottie felt she wasn't reaching June. Her most flirtatious sallies were met with no response whatsoever: June, petrified, would only breathe deep and consciously hold as still as she could. Lottie, frustrated, decided on the direct approach. "I think you're really attractive. Would you like to play with me? What sort of thing do you like to do?" June, cornered again, stammered out, "I don't think I'm ready to have sex in public, so sorry."

Right then, Carol sauntered up to the table and sat down. While June wondered how she could disappear into the bushes without appearing gauche, Lottie greeted Carol by sliding her thigh — which Carol, being a woman

who knew how to act, promptly stroked and admired —
over onto Carol's lap. Lottie, not out of revenge but simple
desire not to waste a perfectly good party, asked Carol:
"How's your dance card tonight? Got room for me?"

Carol asked what was her fancy, and Lottie put out
that she had a yen for a sensitive fist, and Carol said she
would be happy to oblige, just needed to check with Susie
about a plan they had for later. Both happily trotted off,
exchanging a quick body rub as they squeezed through
the door, and June was left to herself. Was she relieved?
Well... not exactly.

Returning to the living room, Lottie was surprised to
see Carol and June both sitting on the windowseat, backs
to the sides, feet in the middle. Lottie had never been
slow to leap on opportunity, so she sashayed across the
room, climbed up on both pairs of feet (neatly trapping
June), and proclaimed: "Here I am!" Carol, being a good
friend of Lottie's and well-versed in the ways of femmes,
called for gloves and lube and firmly pushed Lottie into
June's lap. "Will you hold her for me please?" June
opened her mouth, but nobody waited for her answer,
and next thing, there she was, holding Ms. Lottie's
squirming body. Amazing, thought June, just amazing.
She got a good grip on Lottie, took a deep breath, and
off she went on the ride. June concentrated on keeping
up a good front and trying not to notice several smiling
women who had settled down to watch the action on
the windowseat, while Carol competently went to work

*to turn Lottie on, lube her up and get her off. Omigod,
thought June, how am I going to get through this. I'm
touching this woman's breast and I hardly know her.
Maybe, she thought, I can pretend this is somebody I've
already made love with.*

*Lottie had braced her foot over Carol's shoulder
against the window frame, and was energetically
pushing herself down on Carol's hand. She let out a big
groan as the hand slipped in, and they both starting
fucking hard and loud. June had all she could do to
prevent Lottie from falling onto the floor. Lottie finally
came — loudly, noticed June, very loudly — and June
realized she hadn't breathed for a while, and took a big
gasping breath. All three let their bodies go limp on the
windowseat, and invested a few moments in just feeling
good.*

*Reality eventually asserted itself. Lottie sat up, and
politely offered to fuck Carol in return. Carol said thanks
but no, I promised Susie, and both of them went off in
different directions. June felt like she had fallen into some
other universe — who are these women, anyway?
Although it was kind of fun, and I think I did it okay —
but it's still too much. I think I'd better go to sleep.*

*A day passed. Back at home, Lottie found she could
not stop thinking about June. I know me, she told herself,
and I know when I feel this way I'm just gonna go for it,
so there's no point in agonizing. She called Flash and
discovered that June had flown out of San Francisco that*

morning. Lottie, ever resourceful, got her address and sent her this letter.

Thursday, June 2

Dear June–

It's a beautiful morning up here on my mountain, the sun is streaming through the redwood trees, the sky is very blue with little cloud puffs — yesterday walking up on the ridge I saw a huge jackrabbit. The irises are finished and it's time for morning glories, rhododendrons, and lots of tiny bright exquisite flowers to whom I have not been properly introduced. Do you live in the city? If I make your mouth water for the mountains, will you come visit me?

Who are you anyway? Write me and tell me about yourself. I am particularly interested in how, as a Buddhist, you deal with desire and passion. I've been thinking some about this since we met, and realized that I am not a Buddhist because, although I have gotten a great deal from my connections to Zen, including learning a lot about letting go of desire, my spiritual path is about grasping desire (passion might be a more appropriate word here) as if it were the ox, and riding it as a vehicle to communion with the Dao. I worry that this might not be an acceptable practice to you: although I am used to being various people's version of anathema, I would rather that not be the case with you.

I really like you. I really like the connection we made at Flash's, and I hope we get the chance to explore it further. So write and reveal yourself to me. What are your thoughts about sex, connection, art, nature? What are your fantasies? I really want to know. I bet you dream up some great bedtime stories.

I wish you were here - writing to you is making me nervous and I would like a cuddle. As I read over this letter trying to decide how far to go I realize I have probably already gone too far - oh well, I always do.

Love, Lottie

Eight months and approximately three thousand dollars' worth of phone bills later, not to mention a few impulsive air fares, June put all of her worldly goods in her truck, Lottie flew out to meet her, and they drove across the Great Divide to a sweet little house in the country, where they lived happily ever after.

This is not a typical story of how sluts find partners. Any sexual minority member faces special challenges in partner-finding — and, as a slut or slut wannabe, you are most assuredly a member of a sexual minority. If you're also gay, lesbian, transgender, or interested in a specialized area of sexuality such as crossdressing or S/M, you are doubly or triply challenged.

Many of us have sad, frustrating stories to tell about near-misses: partners who are fine with an open relationship until they start to fall in love, at which point they freak out and demand monogamy... partners who rhapsodize about sexual openness and free love in principle, but can't handle them in reality (Catherine says these remind her of the dog who chases cars all his life, then actually catches one and can't figure out what to do with it)... even partners who are successfully polyamorous, but whose needs, desires and limits simply don't fit together well enough — after all, sex is not the only way we relate.

Yet many people *do* succeed in finding each other, for relationships ranging from casual to lifetime. So, how do you find friends, lovers and potential partners who not only share your values and beliefs — but are also emotionally, intellectually and sexually compatible with you?

Who?

A good place to start is by getting an idea of *who* you're looking for. The trick in making this decision is to be neither too specific nor too vague. If your "who" list basically includes anybody who is breathing and who is willing to have sex with you, we suggest that you are perhaps broadening your field a bit too much. Even if you don't have strong preferences about gender, age, appearance, background or intelligence, you probably do want someone who will not lie to you, steal from you, hurt you or exploit you: basic sanity, honesty and respectfulness are on most of our lists. It is also perfectly fine to acknowledge those preferences that are genuinely important to you: if you prefer men to women, or people your own age to people much older or younger, nobody is going to report you to the Equal Opportunity Commission.

On the other hand, if your "who" list reads like a set of technical specifications — gender, age, weight, height, coloring, mode of dress, educational background, penis size, sexual kinks — we suspect that you may be more interested in making love to your own fantasy than you are to a real, live person. Many of us, unfortunately, are conditioned to react sexually to a rather unrealistic standard of appearance and behavior: porn queens and kings are fun to watch in the movies, but they rarely appear in our living rooms. If you expect your new honey to be gorgeous, loving and highly sexual all the time, you are almost certainly setting yourself up for a lifetime of disappointment — few people can achieve those standards, and nobody can maintain them twenty-four hours a day.

We can't tell you the exact cutoff point at which a healthy preference becomes an unrealistic desire; only you can look inside yourself to do that. We do think that physical appearance, wealth, and social status have very little to do with the person behind them, and if any of those criteria appear high up on your "who" list, you may be a little bit stuck in your fantasy. Try getting to know some people who *don't* meet those criteria. We have a hunch that if you get to know them and like them, you will discover that they have their own unique beauties, just waiting there for someone to notice them.

An important note: even people who *are* gorgeous or rich or busty or whatever don't usually like to feel that their beauty, wallet or breasts are their most attractive quality. Those who partner successfully with them often consider such qualities a happy bonus that have little or nothing to do with why they chose that person in the first place.

WHAT?

What kind of relationship do you want? Do you want someone with whom you can buy a house and raise a family? Someone you can meet once a year for a hot and heavy weekend of role-playing fun? Or "Ms. Right Now"? Knowing what you want up front can prevent a lot of misunderstandings and hurt feelings later.

Ethical sluts do not tell potential sweeties that they're looking for a life partner when, in fact, they're looking to get laid tonight.

Similarly, it's dishonest to swear that all you want is to have a little fun when, in fact, you're mentally measuring him for a tuxedo.

If you're worried that nobody could possibly want what you have to offer, don't be so sure. While it may be harder to find someone who wants to be a secondary partner, or a role-play buddy, or the mother of your children, it is certainly possible — in fact, there are undoubtedly at least a few people out there who are looking for just such a situation.

Trick versus partner is not an either/or situation: there are many, many ways to relate that lie between a one-night stand and marriage. You may not know in advance what kind of relationship will develop with the person who intrigues you tonight, and that person may not fit whatever hole in your life you were looking to fill. Taking people as they come, how they are, here and today, can lead you to wonderful surprises that more than make up for the occasional disappointment. So watch out for your preconceptions, and be ready to approach new people with an open mind and an open heart.

Of course, situations do change. Someone you thought was just an occasional playmate may evolve into a much more important figure in your personal landscape. When this happens — and it has happened to both of us — it is important to keep that person, and anyone else involved, thoroughly briefed on the emotional shifts you're experiencing. It may be that he is feeling the same way toward you, and, Louie, this could be the beginning of a beautiful friendship. On the other hand, he may not. Or he may just not be in a place in his life where a deep emotional commitment is right for him. In any case, treat this changed relationship as though it were a brand-new one — in a way, it is. It may be that the two of you can go on playing in your original, casual manner, or you may have to part for a while to maintain your equilibrium.

WHERE?

Where do sluts gather? What are your best-bet venues for finding the bedmate, playmate or lifemate of your dreams?

Our experience has been that people who are open enough to talk about sexuality may be more interested in other forms of openness, or at least able to hear your desires with respect. So groups, clubs or newspapers organized around sexuality — sexual minorities, group sex, sex education — might be good places to look for kindred spirits.

Additionally, we've found that ethical sluts often enjoy exploring alternative realities (perhaps as novelty-seeking behavior?). Try your local Society for Creative Anachronism, historical re-enactment group (the Renaissance Faire here in Northern California is practically a sluts' trade conference), science fiction conference or role-playing game group.

Another good place to look might be in workshops, seminars and gatherings that have to do with human sexuality or intimacy. While cruising is, understandably, not allowed at some of these activities (people baring their souls are doing difficult work that can be disturbed by having to be on guard against unwanted advances), "graduates" often go on meeting socially long after the actual session is over. There are also several regional and national conferences about sexuality and intimacy, and these are attended by many kindred slutty spirits.

In many of the Internet's sexuality and sexual orientation groups, polyamorists are the majority. In addition to alt.polyamory, a forum devoted exclusively to discussion of the topic, you can find friends in other Usenet newsgroups, private mailing lists, and specialized groups sponsored by Internet service providers. Local adult-oriented computer bulletin boards in many communities are also frequented by a fair number of sluts. Some of these groups allow personal advertising, and some sponsor face-to-face get-togethers. Do be a bit careful, though: as the New Yorker cartoon, showing a mutt happily typing on a keyboard, has it, "On the Internet nobody knows you're a dog." Many people enjoy using the anonymity of the computer screen to experiment with alternate personae, so the 20-year-old masseuse you've been corresponding with may in fact be a 50-year-old truck driver, and the delightfully imaginative slut may in real life be a prude seeking titillation. Still, Catherine (an Internet addict) has found many friends and lovers on the computer, as have countless others of our friends.

You can also cruise the ads in your local newspaper. Modern personal ads usually operate by voicemail: you call a number, hear a recorded message and get an opportunity to record a message of your own, and your phone bill will reflect a per-minute charge for the service. You can answer ads, or put in an ad of your own, or both. Some people run several ads at the same time.

It is customary to get to know people you meet through the Internet or ads in stages, starting with a phone conversation, and then perhaps a date for coffee or dinner, so that you actually get to know the person before you are expected to decide whether or not you want to share sex with them.

Cruising the ads and the Internet are both successful strategies for meeting people. We know of many fine times, and many long-term relationships, that started with a few words in a paper or on a screen.

How?

What do you do once you're face-to-face with a potential playmate? Civilized cruising is a fine art, and one that few people develop overnight. Sex roles make it even harder. Men in this culture are taught to push, to insist, never to take "no" for an answer; women are taught to be coy, to refuse, never to offer an outright "yes." And the more polarized we get in this silly equation, the further we push one another away — with results that range from hurt feelings to date rape.

The good news, though, is that both sets of behavior can be unlearned, and that the more we unlearn them, the less there is to unlearn. When both genders feel free to answer "yes" or "no" with no concern for anything but their own desires, a truer understanding, and a more positive sexuality, can be achieved.

Dossie tells the story of a woman friend of hers back in the '70s who, as an experiment, sat patiently in a singles' bar one night, being approached by many men, until finally one to whom she felt attracted came along and began to flirt. She asked him nicely if he would like to come back to her place and fuck. He swallowed his ice. It took the poor fellow a couple of minutes before he could talk coherently again, and when they actually got to her place he found himself impotent. *That's* how deeply ingrained some of these cultural stereotypes can be.

"No."

Sexual sophisticates tend to give each other a lot of credit for knowing what they want. With this assumption, it becomes easier for your potential partner to make outrageous proposals, because he trusts you to say "no" if you don't want to. It is nobody's task but your own to figure out what you want, and nobody can or will second-guess you. So you are going to have to learn to say "no," and to say "no" easily enough that it won't ruin your evening if you get a couple of unwelcome come-ons. Men as well as women have trouble with this — men are taught that they are always supposed to be up and ready for sex, so if someone comes on to a man when he is not ready, or not interested, it can feel unfamiliar or unmanly to say "no."

When you say "no," do so clearly and kindly. Please do not fall into the trap of putting down people who find you attractive — they must be total idiots to have come onto you, right? Being politely asked is a compliment, not an insult. When we are embarrassed because we need to say no to a polite inquiry, let's just own our own embarrassment. It's not the other person's fault if she thinks you're nifty.

Women have been taught that it is unfeminine to say "no" directly. We are supposed to hint, and this doesn't work. Practice saying "no." Say it to your mirror fifteen times: "No, thank you for the offer, but no." You are not required to produce an excuse or a reason. It would be ridiculous to claim a headache at an orgy. The simple truth is "No, thank you very much, I don't want to."

Women also need to practice saying "yes." Our cultural myth is that the man in a heterosexual transaction pleads with or cons or bullies the woman into saying "yes," or at least refraining from saying "no," and then does whatever he thinks is appropriate. Women need to equalize here, to do more of the choosing, to know what it is that we enjoy and to be able to say what we want in no uncertain terms to whomever we find attractive. And if you are a man whose sexual game plan is more about what you think you are supposed to do to be a good lover than about what you actually want, than you need to learn to say "yes" too. You can expect that this will be more difficult than it looks.

Cruising

Cruising strategies depend a lot on your own gender, and the gender(s) of the people you're seeking.

FOR MEN

Gay men have their own style of cruising, marked by a straightforward approach based on the understanding that most gay men are able to say "no thank you" without much discomfort. Thus, gay men often are able to cruise each other with greater reliance on body language and non-verbal cues than their het brothers.

Successful heterosexual male cruisers, on the other hand, have evolved strategies for conveying interest without coming on too strong, remaining sensitive to verbal and nonverbal cues. Many a man has made the mistake of approaching a woman in the way he thinks he would like to be approached if he were a woman. He may or may not have ever really been approached that way, and he may not appreciate such an approach himself. If you're not sure if women find your approach too heavy-handed, imagine being approached by a large strong gay man using your exact technique, and ask yourself how that feels.

Few women like to be pushed, overwhelmed or not listened to in the arenas of sex and intimacy. Most women are particularly offended by men who push too hard for private get-togethers or phone numbers, who insistently move the conversation back to sexual topics when the woman has tried several times to change the subject, or who touch them, particularly in a sexual, paternalistic or covert way, without permission. Sneaky come-ons are a pain; it works better to simply ask, and if you hear a "no," don't argue.

Dossie remembers going dancing with a group of her gay male friends. In the (mostly gay) disco, a heterosexual man came on to her in a very pushy and obnoxious manner. Dossie's friends were horrified — they'd never seen a man behave like that, not even in the baths.

FOR WOMEN

Most women are not very good at saying "yes," and not very good at saying "no" — *we're* not, and we've been practicing for a long time. We're not sure how things got to this state, where a woman is just supposed to stand there looking adorable until some big strong hunk comes and makes her decision for her, but we don't like it much.

Ask yourself: when was the last time you said "no" to sex? And how did you do it? Was it with a polite, friendly but unmistakable "no thanks"? Or was it with a sort of "not tonight, I've got a headache" or "maybe another time" or "I'll think about it" waffle? We strongly suggest you work out a "no thanks" that feels comfortable to you — Catherine likes "No thanks; you seem nice, but I don't feel a strong chemistry with you." Expecting him to read your mind and somehow know that your "maybe..." means "no" is neither ethical nor slutty.

And again: when was the last time you said "yes" to sex? Simply closing your feminine little eyes and letting him work his will on you is, shall we say, subject to misinterpretation.

Many women, both gay and straight, can benefit greatly from learning to be a bit more assertive in asking for what they want, both during the meeting process and afterwards. If you're used to sipping your drink and waiting for someone to make a move on you, initiating contact yourself may seem terribly awkward, pushy — yes, even slutty — at first. It's also scary as hell to risk rejection like that. It *does* get easier... particularly if you do get rejected a time or two and get a chance to find out that it isn't the end of the world. And, after all, we're not asking you to do anything that men haven't been doing for decades.

So here's the challenge for women: develop at least two scripts for introducing yourself to the man or woman that you find attractive.

"Hi, I'm Susan; who are you?" is just fine for starters. You need a second script to say "I find you attractive, and would you like to: go on a date, come home with me, meet my polyamorous partner..."

FOR COUPLES

If you're in a steady relationship, you and your partner(s) may find yourselves in the situation of cruising *en masse.* Couples cruising has its advantages — if you strike out, you still have someone to go home with. However, many cruisees are not used to the idea of openly non-monogamous relationships, and may get a little freaked out when you come on to them with "Hi, I find you very attractive, and so does my wife." You will find some, however, who actually prefer the safety and built-in boundaries of getting it on with one or both members of an established couple. And isn't that just what you were looking for!

Some couples cruise together for someone to play with in a three-way, while others cruise individually for partners who want to play with one or the other of them. When you cruise on your own, you will eventually have to tell your cruisee that you have a life partner at home. We can't tell you exactly where or how to slip this into the conversation, but we do suggest sooner rather than later.

Whether you cruise individually or together, you need to work out your agreements with each other beforehand. Who is interested in doing what to whom? Where? When? If one of you is looking for someone to hit the mattress with right there that night, and the other wants something permanent ("She followed me home! Can I keep her? Please?"), you may be headed for a major misunderstanding.

We think it's important that those who cruise as couples each have their own social skills. Depending on your partner to do all the work of introductions, conversation, flirtation and negotiation is bad for you and bad for your partner. It may also lead to misunderstandings, since few partners are skilled enough communicators to get across *all* your needs, interests and personality traits.

A pet peeve of many sluts is the couple who treats one or more of the people involved in a disrespectful or objectifying manner. One example is the couple who uses the more conventionally attractive member as "bait" — Catherine remembers once, in a group sex environment, being invited by a man to help stimulate his female partner. As she happily joined the group, she noticed that the man almost immediately shifted his focus from his girlfriend to *her* — ignoring the hapless girlfriend as he grabbed Catherine's breasts. Needless to say, Catherine excused herself immediately from this creepy-feeling scene.

It is disrespectful to treat the third party as some sort of oversized marital aid. Many bisexual women we know are driven to distraction by the "hot bi babe" phenomenon — couples who seek them out, not because they're charming or hot, but because one member of the couple has a fantasy about seeing (or being part of) two women getting it on. Dossie was badly turned off at one group sex environment in which she'd received a sexual invitation from a woman she found attractive. While Dossie's new friend was supposed to be paying attention to Dossie, she was actually beckoning to her husband; he was poised and ready to take his wife's place when Dossie opened her eyes and discovered the substitution. Yuck.

The fundamental rule for cruising as a couple, or getting cruised by a couple, is *respect* for the feelings and relationships of all concerned. You don't want to cruise someone who will try to steal you or your partner for his own, and he doesn't want to be cruised by someone who will use him, withhold information from him or mistreat him. Treat everybody involved with respect, affection and intimacy, and you can reap very special rewards — anything from a warm happy fling to a long-term multiperson relationship.

FOR EVERYONE

The best, most successful and least obnoxious cruisers we know of all orientations are basically friendly, curious folks who like most people and are interested in talking to everyone. If some of the people they talk to turn into potential relationships, so much the better.

Few people of any gender are offended by an honest compliment, an interesting conversational topic, or an appropriate self-revelation. If your cruising skills are weak, ask one or more trusted friends for a critique and practice until you get better at it, or take one of the classes in conversation or flirting that are offered at many Learning Annex-type organizations. Remember, nobody is born knowing how to cruise.

A good conversationalist is usually a successful cruiser, and more often than not a skilled partner as well — because the give-and-take of good conversation, and sensitivity to nonverbal cues, are also important skills for good sex and good relationships.

CHAPTER 2. GROUP SEX, PUBLIC SEX, ORGIES...

Do you want to be an orgy slut? This is a choice. No matter what you may have heard, group sex is not obligatory for open relationships, and we know many fine outrageous sluts who don't attend orgies, or promote three-ways and four-ways in their homes. And we know monogamous couples who frequent public sex environments for the sheer pleasure of playing with each other, in a special and sexy place, complete with an appreciative audience.

If you have ever had a fantasy of being made love to by five people, or having an extra pair of hands to make love with, or lots of hot people to get impulsive with right now, or an appreciative audience that will thrill to your thrashing and screaming in delight... in other words, if you are attracted to the idea of sex parties, this chapter is for you. Here we will tell you what you need to know to have a good time and deal with any difficulties that might come up.

We believe that it is a fundamentally radical political act to deprivatize sex. So much oppression in our culture is based on shame about sex: the oppression of women, of cultural minorities, oppression in the name of the (presumably asexual) family, oppression of sexual minorities. We are all oppressed. We have all been taught, one way or another, that our desires, our bodies, our sexualities, are shameful. What better way to defeat oppression than to get together in communities and celebrate the wonders of sex?

Going to a sex party presents an exciting challenge. It's an opportunity to stretch and grow as we deal with stage fright, performance anxiety, and the wonderful and scary tension of planning and getting ready for elaborated sex in an intensely sexual environment. We are all nervous, and the shared vulnerability adds to the arousal. We love the giddy feeling of conquest when we succeed in overcoming all these obstacles and creating a hot sexual encounter. There's not a lot of room for prudery and shame at an orgy, and when we play in a group of people, we get powerful reinforcement that sex is good and beautiful, and that we are hot and sexy people.

Why Public Sex?

We both enjoy public sex, and regularly attend what we call play parties, environments in which people gather to enjoy a wide variety of kinds of sex with each other. In a highly charged sexual atmosphere, we feel a synergistic kind of arousal when everybody else's excitement feeds our own, and we feel connected to and turned on by all this happy sex that is going on around us.

Group sex offers the chance to try out new partners in a safe environment, surrounded by our friends — we even get the opportunity to check out a person we might be turned on to while they make love with someone else (an audition or advertising, depending on your point of view).

We can learn new sex acts with lots of support: we can watch someone else actually doing a form of sex that we had previously only seen in our fantasies, and we can ask them how they do whatever that is when they are through. We learned many of our safer sex skills at orgies, where rubber barriers are *de rigueur* and there is plenty of support for dealing with awkward bits of latex and maintaining everybody's well-being.

Play parties can help you get over bad body image. As we have pointed out before, people enjoy sex at all ages and in all kinds of bodies, and at any orgy you will see them doing it. One good way to prepare for your first adventure at an orgy is to visit a nude beach or hot spring, if you never have before, to see what real people look like without clothes, and to experience being naked in public yourself. You'll start to see beauty in a lot of bodies that don't look anything like the ones in Playboy or Playgirl, and there's a lot of sensual delight to the feeling of warm sun and gentle breezes on all the parts of our bodies.

It is amazing to us to think, after many years of practicing sex in public, that most people in our culture have never had a chance to watch another person enjoy sex. No wonder we worry so much about our appearance. You will feel much better about how you look, how you perform and who you are, when you have a chance to see real people having real sex. Look around you — every single person is gorgeous when they come. Which is why the orgy can be a perfect stage for the consensual exhibitionist: at the sex party, we all get to be stars and shine our brightest.

Sex clubs are very special environments. San Francisco, where we live, has a delightfully wide choice of orgiastic environments to choose from. There are party spaces for women only, for men only, for couples, for S/M enthusiasts, lovers of drag and costumery, and parties that specialize in just about every sexual practice you can think of — and some that have to be seen to be believed.

Parties may be openly advertised to the public, advertised only in newsletters or at support groups, or may be run by invitation only to a private mailing list. There are public clubs, like the gay men's baths, that are open twenty-four hours a day, seven days a week, and smaller spaces, perhaps an adapted basement recreation room, whose owners host parties once or twice a month. Other congenial groups sponsor small private gatherings in their living rooms.

San Francisco boasts a fair number of "party houses," where one or two stories of a building have been dedicated to the social areas and play rooms for partying. Party houses may rent space to private groups, who might host a party once a month or so for their particular guest list.

The first group sex parties that Dossie attended were held in a communal flat in San Francisco, under the presiding genius of Betty Dodson. Those who lived there were all dedicated to feminism, gay liberation and sexual liberation, and their commune was a conscious experiment to radically change the conditions in which we can enjoy sex. They took out all the doors, and made the loft space upstairs into one unbroken room by getting rid of the furniture. On a typical day, you could find several people on the deck sunbathing nude, some others organizing dinner, two more playing chess, a couple fucking and another person watching them while vibrating. There were larger parties three or four times a year, full of people making love in groups, in twos or singly, with lots of massage, and tantric practitioners chanting "Ommmm" in tune with the ever-present hum of vibrators. This was a private environment, available to the friends and lovers of the six or seven people who lived there.

Public sex environments, whether they're large public clubs or small party houses, have the common function of providing an agreeable space in which you can act sexy. Thus, most have some similarities.

Although the decor and furnishings of group sex environments vary as widely as the human sexual imagination, there are basics that you will find in most party spaces. There will be a door person to check you in, and you may be asked to sign a waiver of liability. There will be a social area, with places to sit and talk and meet people, usually with a small buffet of snacks and beverages. Sex does not usually take place in the social area. There will be lockers or coat racks or shelves or some place to put your street clothes, and either change into party costume or simply disrobe. Some parties are mostly naked, others feature a dazzling array of clothes for every sexual fantasy. There will be provisions for cleanliness, bathrooms and showers. Then there will be the play room or rooms.

Play rooms vary from tiny cubicles, often set up as mazes, with a small bed just big enough to fuck on, to large rooms with mirrored walls and upholstered floors for puppy piles, group gropes, and other orgiastic activities. There may be hot tubs, steam rooms and gardens for you to cruise and relax in. There may be an area for dancing. There is often music with a very strong beat, to enhance your natural rhythm and to give a sense of aural privacy so you won't be distracted by the noise of others. The lights will be low, and often red or orange, so we all can look a little tan and perhaps a little sexier. There may be rooms with furniture imaginatively designed to have sex on, like medical examining tables or slings, mirrored beds or dungeons for S/M fantasies, or perhaps a giant waterbed for those who like to make waves.

Play party spaces tend to form communities. People try out the various parties in their area, and usually return to one or two groups that they find congenial. As people get to know each other, and share the special intimacy of sexual connection, they often become friends and form extended families. It is not unusual at all to find a sex party club hosting a benefit for a member who has had an accident or a major illness. These are communities, and communities take care of their own.

Group Sex Etiquette

We know they didn't teach you in school how to behave at an orgy, and we bet your mother didn't teach you either.

There is a particular etiquette needed for public sex environments, since everyone in them has let down some of their customary boundaries in order to get closer to each other. Social boundaries usually serve the purpose of keeping people at a predictable distance, so we all feel safe in our own personal space. Group sex poses the challenge of figuring out how to feel safe and comfy while getting up close and very intimate with a whole bunch of presumably nice, sexy people — so new boundaries must be developed, learned and respected, or no one will feel safe enough to play.

Many party houses show you a list of rules as you come in, or post them on the wall. Read them. They will make sense. Most places specify the level of safer sex precautions they require, and provide condoms, rubber gloves, lubricants, dental dams, and so on. Even if you and your partner are fluid-bonded, you may be asked, or feel it is polite, to use latex barriers in a public environment. Ethical sluts obey the rules of the parties they choose to attend.

Responsible voyeurism is a must. You may watch what people do in public places, but always from a respectful distance. If the participants are aware of your presence, you are too close. Whether or not it is okay to masturbate while watching varies from place to place, but it's always polite to keep your own excitement discreet enough that you don't distract the good folks who are putting on such a nice show —

they are probably not actually doing it for you, anyway. Also be aware that when you are close to people who are playing, they can hear you – this is not an appropriate place to tell your friend all about how awful your boss is, or your recent experiences at the proctologist.

The boundary between social/talk space and play space is very important – when you enter play space, you enter into a different state of consciousness that tends to get you out of your intellect and into your body very quickly. Too much talking in play space can yank you back into everyday, verbal, nonsexual awareness.

Cruising is active, but must not be intrusive. Ideally, a respectful request receives a respectful response, which means it's okay to ask, and if the answer is "no, thank you," that has to be okay too. Remember, people who come to orgies are pretty sophisticated, and they are here because they know what they want. And if that person you found attractive doesn't want to play with you right now, that's okay, take it easy and find someone else.

Cruising at group sex parties is not that different from elsewhere, although perhaps more honest and to the point. Usually, you start with introducing yourself as a person: "Hi, I'm Dick, what's your name?" is way preferable to "Hi, do you like my big dick?" People will talk for a bit, flirt a little, and then ask quite directly "Would you like to play with me?" When the answer is yes, negotiation follows: "What do you like to do? Is there anything you don't like? Let's check that we both mean the same thing by safer sex, and by the way, I have this fantasy..."

NON-VERBAL COMMUNICATION

Cruising by body language also can work, as long as you are willing to be relaxed about any misunderstandings that may arise. We believe that it is important to learn how to put what you want into words, so you have an option for absolutely clear communication. Then you can pursue nonverbal cruising if you like it, knowing your good communication skills will back you up if you need them.

Body language is about catching someone's eye, exchanging a smile, moving your body closer — always checking the response. If you catch his eye and he turns his back, well, there's your answer. If you move into her personal space and she moves closer, there's another answer. It helps to initiate touch on a relatively neutral part of the body — a shoulder, a hand — and again, does the person move away, or closer? If he freezes, it's probably a good idea to communicate with words.

GENDER DIFFERENCES

We live in a society where people learn some pretty warped ideas about sex. Women learn that they are not supposed to be sexual without falling in love, men learn that sex is a commodity that you get from a woman, men may even believe that women themselves are commodities. Group sex only works when everybody is acknowledged as a person. Nobody likes being treated like a thing. To avoid such problems, most group sex environments that include both men and women restrict the number of single men who are invited, or insist that no man is welcome without a female escort. This is a sad last resort for dealing with an unpleasant reality, and we quite agree that it is unfair that men of good will get penalized for the intrusive behavior of men who evidently don't know any better. But that's how it is, and the only way we are going to change it is to work on our own behavior and teach our brothers what we learn.

Cruising is different by gender, and those differences become very visible when you compare gay men's environments to lesbian orgies, and see how they are similar and different to hetero or bisexual groups. Gay men seem to feel safer with anonymous sex, and gay male cruising at baths or clubs is often nonverbal. One man might catch another's eye, smile, walk across the room, touch a shoulder and then embrace, with little or no verbal communication. Lesbians are more cautious, and tend to talk a great deal before moving into the playroom and actually getting down.

Women in all group sex environments tend to be less open than men to anonymous sex, and to prefer some communication and personal connection first. Perhaps this is because women have had serious reasons to feel less than safe around sex with strangers, and need some reassurance that this is a safe person to play with. There are no rights and wrongs to this situation, or what wrong there is exists in our history, which we can't very well change. What is important is that everyone, male, female or transgendered, straight, bi or gay, has a right to feel safe in order to get free to enjoy sex.

ESTABLISHING CONSENT

Consent is an absolute requirement. Naive people sometimes assume that when two or three or four people are already having sex, it is okay to just join in and start fondling somebody. Well, it isn't, because you didn't ask, and because you don't know what these people want, or what their limits are. So you might do the wrong thing, and the people you tried to join will have to stop whatever they are having so much fun doing to deal with you, and then they will be justifiably angry. At you. And how are you going to get consent from people in the middle of a hot fuck? Tap them on the shoulder and say, "Will you please stop a moment so I can ask if I can join you?" There is just about no way to join a sexual scene that has already started unless you are already lovers with all the people involved, and even then you should be careful. Respect for boundaries, as we have said before, is mandatory if everyone is going to feel safe enough to play freely and without constraint. Don't be the person who makes the environment unsafe.

If you are playing at a party and someone invades your space, you are quite right to tell them to move away. It is also appropriate to let your host know about intrusive people and pushy come-ons — party hosts develop skills to talk with people about appropriate behavior, explain why the etiquette is as it is, and if the person will not learn, the host has the power to remove that person from the guest list.

WATCH YOUR EXPECTATIONS

Most people approach their first group sex party with a virtual brainstorm of fears, fantasies and wild expectations about what might, or worse yet, might not happen. We strongly recommend that you get a grip on yourself, acknowledge that you actually don't know what is going to happen, and go to the party with the expectation that you will be proud of yourself if you manage to walk in the door. If you stay for an hour and watch, you get a gold star. If you manage to introduce yourself to someone and hold a conversation, give yourself a medal of honor.

Going to an orgy is very challenging. Expect to be nervous. Expect to worry. Expect a fashion crisis, and allow at least two hours to get dressed. Many parties specify when doors are open, and close them at eleven or so, because otherwise all these nervous people will arrive after midnight, having finally decided to wear something, and too late to warm up for play before the party is over. So be easy on yourself.

Dress to look good and be comfortable — it's bad enough to have your stomach churning, you don't need your shoes pinching. Go with the goal of making a few acquaintances and getting familiar with the scene and your reactions to it. If you do get inspired to play, and find someone who wants to play with you, that's fine, and if you don't, that's fine too.

COUPLES AT THE ORGY

Deal with your relationship before you go to the party. This is important. Are you going as a couple, to show off your incredible sexiness? Are you cruising for thirds and fourths? Or are you going as two separate individuals, to meet people and share sex with them? If one of you connects with a hot number, is the other welcome to join in? Do you need your partner's agreement before you play with anyone? Are you committed to going home together, or is it okay for one or the other of you to sleep out, and if both want to, what about the babysitter? The reason you decide all this in advance is that it is way too embarrassing to have a disagreement about this sort of thing in public, so if you do disagree, you are likely to get really angry and make a big unhappy mess.

Two friends of ours got locked in a disagreement about going to sex parties. They both wanted to go, but one wanted to go and play with the other, and the other wanted to play the field. What to do? Well, there are parties at least once a month around here, so they decided to go one month as a couple to do things together, and the next to support each other in separate and seriously intense cruising.

We like to watch couples make love with each other at parties — you can see the intimacy, and how well they know each other's ways, how beautifully they fit together, how exquisitely orchestrated lovemaking can become with years of practice. We like it as a fine experience for the voyeur, and because we can learn a lot from watching people who are experts on each other. We like to point out that showing off this wondrous beauty is also excellent advertising for the next time when you come to the party ready to welcome new partners.

Play parties can also offer you the opportunity to process fears and jealousies about your partner. How does it feel to watch your partner make love with another person? Is it really awful? You might be surprised to find yourself feeling pretty neutral, like "Gee, I thought that would bother me but actually it doesn't!" You might like the chance to observe your lover, how powerful she looks when she thrusts, how sweet he looks when he comes. It might even turn you on. Some couples find that group sex can rev up their sex life at home, by providing a lot of stimulus, new ideas to try out, and the motivation and energy to make your life at home as hot as an orgy.

Buttons and biases

Expect to get buttons pushed. Expect to discover your biases. At a group sex party you will share unprecedented intimacy with a bunch of strangers, and sometimes that will be difficult. You might start into a threeway with your girlfriend and another man, which seems like a hot idea but might turn out to push some buttons. Yeah, we know, you set out to both make love to her, but there you are, with another man, being sexual, and probably in physical contact, and how does that feel?

We like to attend pansexual group sex parties, which means that attendees may identify as gay or lesbian or bisexual or hetero or transgendered, but are generally comfortable and happy to play side-by-side with people whose desires may be entirely different than their own. We are always running into issues about the unfamiliar: the lesbian who has never been naked in the presence of men, much less gotten fucked; the gay man who fears judgment from women, or violence from straight men; the transgendered woman who gets to wonder if that person who is so attracted to her knows what she's got under her skirt, and does she care, and if she cares what is she going to do?

Whatever your prejudices are — the people at this party are too old, too young, too male, too female, too queer, too straight, too fat, too thin, too white, too ethnic, whatever — it really is good for you to learn to get bigger than your biases.

EVERYTHING EMBARRASSING YOU NEVER THOUGHT OF DOING IN PUBLIC

In our fantasies, we all come together as smoothly as Fred and Ginger, carried away by the music on a rising tide of passion — and sometimes it will be like that. But you probably will need to practice first, just like Fred and Ginger. Your erection might refuse to cooperate as you near the moment of truth, especially when you suddenly remember you need to put a condom on it. Orgasm might be more difficult to focus on in a noisy environment with an unfamiliar partner — are you going to fake one? What if you set out to play with someone and you can't find your turn-on?

A young roommate of Dossie's once wound up in bed with both her current and her previous lover in an unplanned episode of lust run amok. Courtesy of inadequate soundproofing and a good imagination, Dossie knew what was going on and was wondering how they were doing when Kenny, the current boyfriend, staggered into the kitchen. "Dossie," he pleaded, "I don't know what to do! Help!" She said, "Don't forget to breathe, this is not a contest, this is about doing what feels good." He muttered it like a mantra, "Breathe, no contest, feel good, breathe, no contest..." squared his shoulders and gamely returned to the fray.

So if you find yourself internally panicking, we encourage you to breathe. Slow down. Remember that this is not a race, and you are not in a hurry. This is also not the Olympics, you have nothing to prove — you and your new friend are setting out to do things that feel good with your bodies. Touch feels good. Stroking feels good. Taking time feels good. Slow down enough so that you can truly feel what you are doing. Worrying about the future will not help you get there: focus on what you are feeling in the present. Erections and orgasms might come, might go, but you can never go wrong by doing what feels good.

The noise and hectic energy of a party can lead people to rush when slowing down is the best way to connect with your turn-on. People don't get turned on by magic, at least not very often, or very reliably. And different people are turned on in very different ways. A very important kind of self-knowledge will come in handy at these times: know what turns you on. Whether it's biting on the neck or sucking on the backs of knees, when you know what gets your juices flowing you can ask for it, and then your play partner will know what turns you on, and feel freer to tell you what turns her or him on, and before you know it there you all are, completely turned on and floating down the river of unbridled lust.

CONCLUSION: A SLUT UTOPIA

PARADIGMS AND PLURALISM

Earlier in this book, we discussed the paradigms on which our relationships, and our beliefs about our relationships, are based. We also talked about the ways in which our vision is limited by the prevailing beliefs of our culture, and the ways in which those limits can prevent us from expanding our sexuality, our lifestyle, our families and our love.

Monism is the belief that all processes, structures and relationships can be reduced to a single element, that everything can eventually be explained by one governing principle[13]. When we ask a question, we often assume that there must be only one answer, and thus that if there's more than one answer then our task is not finished and our question not really answered. This is monist thinking. When we look at how we run our relationships and families, for example, monism leads us to believe that there is some single best way, some ideal marriage, and our goal is to get as close to that ideal as possible. Monism leads us to believe that all possibilities can be ranked on a hierarchy like in the old Sears catalog — good, better, best — and that only the best one counts. When we constantly compare our lives and our selves to a single ideal, and take off points for any way in which we differ from that ideal, we discount ourselves constantly, and we never discover our true value.

Dualism is the theory that everything comes in pairs, like mind and body, black and white, or, as computers would have it, 0 and 1. Dualists describe the world in terms of divisions, of barriers: between mind and body, man and women, straight and gay, good and bad. We often imagine that these pairs are opposed, like good and evil. Dualistic thinking in the form of adversarialism dominates our courts, our politics and our talk shows, with some crazy results: for instance, some people believe that anyone who enjoys sex outside of marriage must be attacking traditional ways of relating; our president has signed the "Defense of Marriage Act." Anything that is different must be opposed, must be the enemy.

Dualism may lead to the belief that you can't love more than one person, or that you can't love in different ways, or that you have a finite capacity for love — that "many" must somehow be opposed to "one," or that your only options are "in love" and "out of love," with no allowance for different degrees or kinds of love.

Pluralism is the open-ended view, the multi-valued system, that refuses the intellectual simplification of reducing everything down to one or two, and insists on seeing, and valuing, everything that there is. To the pluralist, all existence, and certainly each single person's life, is important — so there can be as many ways to be sexual as there are to be human, and all of them valid. There are lots of ways to relate, to love, to express gender, to form families, to be in the world, to be human. And all of those ways are wonderful.

In order to unlearn monogamy and liberate our sexuality, we need to uproot the arbitrary limitations to our thinking and seeing that have been imposed on our minds by previous philosophies. When we manage to get bigger than our programmed judgments, we become able to see beyond: beyond worrying about how do we look, how's our performance, our partner's performance, our fantasy of our partner's other lover's performance, all our beliefs that we are not really okay. When we learn to transcend those conditioned responses that limit our actions, our thinking and our very awareness, we can free ourselves to be fully conscious of all the wonderful variety and diversity that there is right now in the world, right here, in the present, available to us.

Thus pluralism and sluthood can become a path to transcendence, a freeing of the mind and spirit as well as the body, a way of being in the world that allows expanded awareness, spiritual growth and — not incidentally — *really* good sex.

SLUT UTOPIA

We believe that when we examine the issues that limit our relationships and our understanding of how we might be, we are essentially planning for a society that is appropriate to the way many people live today — that meets our need for change and growth while it feeds our fundamental desire for belonging and family.

We believe that monogamy will continue to thrive as it always has, a perfectly valid choice for those who truly choose it. We don't think it's much of a choice when you are forbidden to choose anything else. We want to open our vision to accommodate monogamy as well as a plethora of other options — to plan for family and social structures that have growing room, that will continue to stretch and adapt, that we can fit to our needs into the future. We believe that new forms of families are evolving now, and will continue to evolve, not to supplant the nuclear family but to supplement it with an abundance of additional ideas about how you might choose to structure your family. We want to create a whole world of choices for sex and love, for family and community. We want to set you free to invent the society you want to live in.

Our vision of utopia has free love, in all its forms, as the foundation of our beliefs about reality, about possibility, about staying in the moment and planning the future. We believe that sexual freedom helps us to see our lives as they really are, with the honesty to perceive ourselves clearly and the fluidity to let us move onward as our needs alter, as a changing and growing self with changing and growing partners in a changing and growing world.

We see ethical sluthood leading us to a world where we respect and honor each individual's boundaries more than we honor any preconceived set of rules about how their boundaries ought to be.

And in expanding our sexual lives, we foresee the development of an advanced sexuality, where we can become both more natural and more human. Sex really is a physical expression of a whole lot of stuff that has no physical existence: love and joy, deep emotion, intense closeness, profound connection, spiritual awareness, incredibly good feelings, sometimes even ecstasy. In our utopia, intellect is not a trap that we get stuck in, but an honored tool we use to discover and access all the parts of ourselves, and give form to our experience. We free our animal selves by opening our intellects to awareness of our bodies, and when we are no longer stuck in our intellects we become more like spirit: intuitive, experiencing the joy of life for the simple sake of experiencing, in communion with ourselves, with each other, and beyond.

Our favorite sex fantasy: sexual abundance

We want everyone to be free to express love in every possible way. We want to create a world where everyone has plenty of what they need:

of community, of connection, of touch and sex and love. We want our children to be raised in an expanded family, a connected village within urban alienation, where there are enough adults who love them and each other, so that there is plenty of love and attention and nurturance, more than enough to go around. We want a world where the sick and aging are cared for by people who love them, where resources are shared by people who care about each other.

We dream of a world where no one is driven by desires they have no hope of fulfilling, where no one suffers from shame for their desires, or embarrassment about their dreams, where no one is starving from the lack of sex. We dream of a world where no one is limited by rules that dictate that they must be less of a person, and less of a sexual person, than they have the capacity to be.

We dream of a world where nobody gets to vote on your life choices, or who you choose to love, or how you choose to express that love, except yourself and your lovers. We dream of a time and a place where we will all be free to publicly declare our love, for whoever we love, however we love them.

And may we all look forward to a lifetime of dreams come true.

Chapter Notes

1   Edna St. Vincent Millay, Collected Poems, Harper & Row, NY, no date. Edna is also responsible for another slut favorite: "My candle burns at both ends/It will not last the night./But ah my foes and oh my friends/It makes a lovely light."

2   Wardell B. Pomeroy, Dr. Kinsey and the Institute for Sex Research, Harper & Row Publishers, New York, 1973. Page 316.

3   Jane Austen, Pride and Prejudice, New American Library, 1988.

4   Sigmund Freud, Three Contributions to the Theory of Sex, E.P. Dutton & Co., Inc., New York, 1962 (orig. 1905), p. 51.

5   Dossie Easton & Catherine A. Liszt, The Bottoming Book: Or, How To Get Terrible Things Done To You By Wonderful People, Greenery Press, San Francisco, 1994.

6   Wilhelm Reich, Sex/Pol, Random House, New York, 1966. Throughout these essays, and in The Mass Psychology of Fascism, Reich develops a sophisticated analysis of the role of sexual repression in enforcing obedience to authority in classist, capitalist and fascist societies.

7   James Ramey, Ph.D., Intimate Friendships, Prentice Hall, Englewood Cliffs, New Jersey, 1976.

8   William H. Masters, M.D., & Virginia E. Johnson, Human Sexual Response, Little, Brown & Co., Boston, 1966, pps. 198–201.

9   see Bernard Zilbergeld, Ph.D., <u>The New Male Sexuality</u>, Bantam Books, New York, 1992, and Lonnie Barbach, Ph.D.: <u>For Yourself: The Fulfillment of Female Sexuality</u>, New American Library, New York, 1991.

10   Neil Young, "Love Is a Rose," Silver Fiddle, 1975

11   Kahlil Ghibran, <u>The Prophet</u>, Alfred A. Knopf, New York, 1968, p. 52

12   Adapted from <u>How to Talk So Kids Wil Listen and Listen So Kids Will Talk</u>, Adele Faber & Elaine Mazlish, Avon Books, New York, 1980

13   <u>Random House Dictionary of the English Language</u>, Unabridged, Random House, New York, 1971, p. 925.

BIBLIOGRAPHY

Dr. Deborah M. Anapol, Polyamory: The New Love Without Limits, IntiNet Resource Center, San Rafael, CA, 1997.

Dr. George R. Bach and Peter Wyden: The Intimate Enemy: How to Fight Fair In Love and Marriage, Avon Books, New York, 1968.

Lonnie Barbach, Ph.D.: For Each Other: Sharing Sexual Intimacy, Signet Books, New York, 1984.

Lonnie Barbach, Ph.D.: For Yourself: The Fulfillment of Female Sexuality, New American Library, New York, 1991.

Kate Bornstein: Gender Outlaw: On Men, Women and the Rest of Us, Routledge, New York, 1994.

Pat Califia: Public Sex, Cleis Press, Pittsburgh, 1994.

Pat Califia: Sapphistry, Naiad Press, Tallahassee, 1988.

Stephanie Covington, Ph.D., Awakening Your Sexuality: A Guide for Recovering Women, Harper, San Francisco, 1991.

Hayden Curry, Denis Clifford & Robin Leonard: A Legal Guide for Lesbian and Gay Couples, Ninth Edition, Nolo Press, Berkeley, 1996.

Betty Dodson, Ph.D.: Sex for One, Crown Trade Paperbacks, New York, 1996.

Sigmund Freud: <u>Three Contributions to the Theory of Sex</u>, E.P. Dutton & Co., Inc., 1962 (originally published in 1905).

J. Patrick Gannon, Ph.D.: <u>Soul Survivors: A New Beginning for Adults Abused As Children</u>, Prentice-Hall, New York, 1989.

The Institute for Advanced Study of Human Sexuality: <u>The Complete Guide to Safe Sex</u>, Specific Press, Beverly Hills, California, 1987.

Greg Kettelback: <u>How to Make Love While Conscious: Sex and Sobriety</u>, Harper, San Francisco, 1993.

Kevin Lano and Claire Parry, editors: <u>Breaking the Barriers to Desire: Polyamory, Polyfidelity and Non-monogamy — New Approaches to Multiple Relationships</u>, Five Leaves Publications, Nottingham, UK, 1995.

Harriet Goldhor Lerner, Ph.D.: <u>The Dance of Anger</u>, Harper & Row, New York, 1986.

Harriet Goldhor Lerner, Ph.D.: <u>The Dance of Intimacy</u>, Harper & Row, New York, 1989.

Dr. Harold Litten: <u>The Joy of Solo Sex</u>, Factor Press, Mobile, Alabama, 1993.

JoAnn Loulan: <u>Lesbian Sex</u>, Spinsters/Aunt Lute, San Francisco, 1984.

Dr. Patricia Love: <u>Hot Monogamy</u>, Penguin, New York, 1994.

Robert K. Moffet: <u>Tantric Sex</u>, Berkeley Publishing Corp., New York, 1974.

Jack Morin, Ph.D.: <u>The Erotic Mind</u>, Harper Perennial, New York, 1996.

Ryam Nearing: Loving More: The Polyfidelity Primer, LovingMore Publishing, Boulder, CO, 1996

Tuppy Owens: Safer Planet Sex: The Handbook, A K Press Distribution, 1994

Carol Queen: Exhibitionism for the Shy, Down There Press, San Francisco, 1995.

James Ramey, Ph.D.: Intimate Friendships, Prentice Hall, Engle-wood Cliffs, New Jersey, 1976.

Riley K. Smith, M.A., and Tina B. Tessina, M.A.: How to Be a Couple & Still Be Free, Newcastle Publishing Co., Inc., North Hollywood, CA, 1987.

Kenneth Ray Stubbs, Ph.D., The Sensuous Lovers' Guide, Secret Garden, Larkspur, CA, 1986.

Kenneth Ray Stubbs, Ph.D., Editor, Women of the Light: The New Sacred Prostitute, Secret Garden, Larkspur, CA, 1984.

Celeste West: Lesbian Polyfidelity, Booklegger Press, 1995.

Cathy Winks & Anne Semans, The Good Vibrations Guide to Sex, Cleis Press, San Francisco, 1994.

Bernard Zilbergeld, Ph.D., The New Male Sexuality, Bantam Books, New York, 1992.

RESOURCES FOR SLUTS

MAGAZINES AND PERIODICALS

Green Egg
P.O. Box 1542
Ukiah, CA   95482

These folks also offer various books and tapes on polyamory and polyfidelity, and sponsor an annual conference

LovingMore
P.O. Box 4358
Boulder, CO 80306
Phone/FAX: 303/543-7540 Mountain Time
Ryam@lovemore.com
http://www.lovemore.com.

CLUBS, WORKSHOPS AND OTHER RESOURCES

Alt.polyamory is a medium-traffic Internet Usenet newsgroup which focuses specifically on issues surrounding open and non-monogamous relationships. While the majority of posters are interested in long-term committed multipartner relationships, other posters represent other forms of slutdom. Its FAQ (Frequently Asked Questions) gets posted about once a month, or you can read it on the Web at http://www.cs.ruu.nl/wais/html/na-dir/polyamory/faq.html. Another Usenet group, alt.personals.poly, is a good place for personal ads if you're seeking partners for non-monogamous relationships or fun.

If you're gay or lesbian, these are good places to start in your search for sluts interested in same-sex relationships.

The Bob Damron Guidebook
The Damron Company
P.O. Box 422458
San Francisco, CA 94142-2458

National Gay Yellow Pages
Box 292, Village Station
New York, NY 10014

If you're bisexual, try:

Bisexual Resource Center
P.O. Box 639
Cambridge, MA 02140
(617) 338-9595
brc@norn.org   http://norn.org/pub/other-orgs/brc/index.html

This organization puts on a series of weekend-long intensive workshops on Sex, Love and Intimacy. We hear they are excellent.

Human Awareness Institute
1720 South Amphlett Blvd., Ste. 120
San Mateo, CA 94402 (800) 800-4117 info@hai.org

This organization offers courses, in various locations nationwide, designed to help men and women expand their erotic boundaries and deepen the connection between the sexual and the spiritual.

Body Electric
(510) 653-1594

This organization offers workshops and individualized consultation on polamory, sexual healing, sacred sexuality and related topics. It also sells a variety of books, magazines and videotapes on polyamory and spirituality.

Sacred Space Institute

P.O. Box 4322

San Rafael, CA 94913

(415) 507-1739

pad@well.com

If you are primarily heterosexual, and looking for friendly and uncommitted sex outside a primary relationship, the swing community may be your home. These folks sponsor various events and vacations, and publish a directory of swing clubs worldwide.

North American Swing Club Association (NASCA)

P.O. Box 7128

Buena Park, CA 90622

(714) 229-4870

RESOURCES THAT CAN HELP WITH PROBLEMS

Kink-Aware Professionals is a list of physicians, therapists, attorneys and other professionals who are open to alternative sexualities and lifestyles. E-mail race@bannon.com, check their website at http:// www.bannon.com/~race/kap, or send a self-addressed business-sized envelope with two regular stamps on it to:

Kink-Aware Professionals

c/o Race Bannon

584 Castro St. #518

San Francisco, CA 94114-2500

The National STD Hotline can answer your questions and refer you to resources about sexually transmitted diseases and conditions. Their toll-free number is (800) 227-8922.

The National Domestic Violence Hotline can help if anyone in your relationship is violent or abusive. Their toll-free number is (800) 333-SAFE.

Planned Parenthood can help you with issues surrounding birth control, pregnancy (wanted or unwanted), and sexually transmitted diseases and conditions. Call their national toll-free number at (800) 344-4435 to learn the location of the office nearest you.

GENERAL RESOURCES

This university-based organization maintains a detailed, thorough, and up-to-date database of sexuality-related information. Write them, or better yet check their website, for good current information about resources for sluts.

> Society for Human Sexuality
> University of Washington
> SAO 141
> Box 352238
> Seattle, WA 98195
> http://weber.u.washington.edu/~sfpse/

This free switchboard is staffed on weekdays from 3 p.m. to 9 p.m. Pacific time with trained volunteers who can answer sex-related questions and refer you to groups which are appropriate to your needs.

> San Francisco Sex Information
> (415) 989-7374

OTHER BOOKS FROM GREENERY PRESS

GENERAL SEXUALITY

... But I Know What You Want: 25 Sex Tales for
the Different
James Williams $13.95

The Ethical Slut: A Guide to Infinite Sexual
Possibilities
Dossie Easton & Catherine A. Liszt $16.95

Fantasy Made Flesh: The Essential Guide to
Erotic Roleplay
Deborah Addington $13.95

A Hand in the Bush: The Fine Art of Vaginal
Fisting
Deborah Addington $13.95

Paying For It: A Guide By Sex Workers for
Their Customers
edited by Greta Christina $13.95

Phone Sex: Oral Skills and Aural Thrills
Miranda Austin $15.95

Sex Disasters... & How to Survive Them
C. Moser, Ph.D., M.D. & Janet W. Hardy $16.95

Tricks... To Please a Man
Tricks... To Please a Woman
both by Jay Wiseman $13.95 ea.

When Someone You Love Is Kinky
Dossie Easton & Catherine A. Liszt $15.95

BDSM/KINK

The Compleat Spanker
Lady Green $12.95

Erotic Slavehood: A Miss Abernathy Omnibus
Christina Abernathy $15.95

Erotic Tickling
Michael Moran $13.95

Family Jewels
Hardy Haberman $12.95

Flogging
Joseph W. Bean $12.95

Intimate Invasions: The Ins and Outs of Erotic
Enema Play
M.R. Strict $13.95

The Kinky Girl's Guide to Dating
Luna Grey $16.95

The (new and improved) Loving Dominant
John & Libby Warren $16.95

The New Bottoming Book
The New Topping Book
Dossie Easton & Janet W. Hardy $14.95 ea.

Play Piercing
Deborah Addington $13.95

Radical Ecstasy: SM Journeys to Transcendence
Dossie Easton & Janet W. Hardy $16.95

The Seductive Art of Japanese Bondage
Midori, photographs by Craig Morey $27.95

The Sexually Dominant Woman: A Workbook
for Nervous Beginners
Lady Green $11.95

SM 101: A Realistic Introduction
Jay Wiseman $24.95

21st Century Kinkycrafts
edited by Janet Hardy $19.95

TOYBAG GUIDES:
A Workshop In A Book $9.95 each

Canes and Caning, *by Janet Hardy*

Clips and Clamps, *by Jack Rinella*

Dungeon Emergencies & Supplies, *by Jay Wiseman*

Erotic Knifeplay, *by Miranda Austin & Sam Atwood*

Foot and Shoe Worship, *by Midori*

High-Tech Toys, *by John Warren*

Hot Wax and Temperature Play, *by Spectrum*

Medical Play, *by Tempest*